SUSHI
MADE SIMPLE

ATSUKO IKEDA

SUSHI
MADE SIMPLE

From classic wraps and rolls to modern bowls and burgers

Photography by YUKI SUGIURA

RYLAND PETERS & SMALL
LONDON • NEW YORK

CONTENTS

INTRODUCTION

With sushi restaurants opening and thriving in so many towns and cities, sushi has become an everyday food for many people. However, when you try to make something delicious at home that you have eaten in a restaurant, it can be difficult to work out how to do it properly and exactly which ingredients to use. With *Sushi Made Simple* you will learn just how to do this. In this, my first book, I would like to share with you the traditional skills of sushi-making, teach you authentic but modern recipes and explain some aspects of Japanese culture too.

I have been teaching Japanese cookery lessons for almost 10 years in Atsuko's Kitchen – my cooking school in London – and sushi-making has always been one of my most popular classes. One of the things that surprises my students the most is how versatile sushi is: it can be quick and easy and perfect for a lunchbox, or more meticulous and time-consuming for a special occasion. They all leave the course amazed at what they have accomplished.

The secret to good sushi lies in its simplicity, and within this book I present new approaches to making sushi, with recipes using both traditional methods and techniques and modern variations. The book guides you step by step through the entire sushi-making process, from advising you on the essential tools to stocking your pantry and choosing ingredients. The basic techniques section shows you all the construction tricks, including preparing fish, cutting vegetables, cooking sushi rice and building the various types of sushi rolls.

I was born on the Japanese island of Kyushu – also known as the 'food island' – and I always loved food and cooking. My mother and grandmother were both good cooks and shared their knowledge with me. However, it was only when I left Japan and spent most of a year sailing across the Atlantic to the Galapagos Islands that this passion took on a new dimension: we fished every day and I started to give cooking classes wherever we stopped to people who initially thought of Japanese cuisine as arduous and tricky. When I began teaching in London in 2008, I wanted to take away the mystery of Japanese cuisine and show that with knowledge, guidance and practice, it can be made by all. I have taught thousands of students who now cook Japanese meals and make sushi at home, even including my Italian husband Michele who I met in my class at the very beginning of my teaching career. It has become my lifetime mission!

Enjoy the sushi journey throughout this book and I hope you will gain the confidence to experiment with your own sushi making.

TYPES OF SUSHI

DECONSTRUCTED

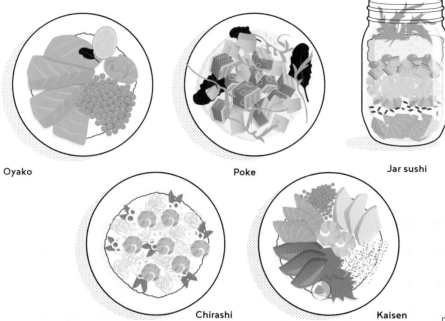

Oyako

Poke

Jar sushi

Chirashi

Kaisen

Futomaki

Temaki

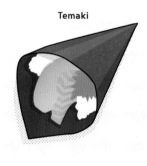

SUSHI FAMILY

CREATIVE MOULDED

Cake

Bomb

Christmas

Burger

Doughnut

Sandwich

Nigiri

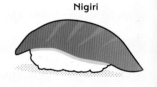

Oshi sushi

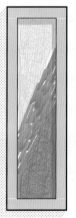

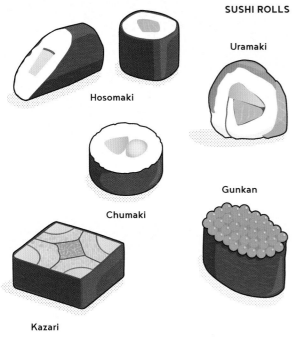

SUSHI ROLLS

Hosomaki

Uramaki

Chumaki

Gunkan

Kazari

TRADITIONAL MOULDED

Inari

Battera

Chakin

Temari

Suko sushi

Mosaic

THE THREE SUSHI PRINCIPLES

Finding the golden balance is paramount in making any dish. With sushi, you can create endless variations by combining sushi rice with different sorts of toppings or fillings. Bear in mind the following balance of three principles, as this will inspire ideas and make your sushi-making easy and successful!

COLOUR BALANCE
red, yellow, green, brown, white, black

Eat with your eyes! Rainbow colours or matching colours work well visually and add nutritional value. And most of all, you'll enjoy playing with colours when creating your sushi.

FLAVOUR BALANCE
sweet, sour, salty, bitter, umami, spicy

Harmonise all these flavours in each mouthful for a satisfying meal. Different combinations of ingredients, and the choice of dipping sauces and other condiments, create the depth of flavours and the overall balance. Soy sauce and wasabi are probably the most well-known sauces and condiment, but there are plenty of others you can use.

TEXTURE BALANCE
crunchy, crisp, chewy, sticky, creamy, crumbly

So many textures make for so many sushi possibilities! Even adding some crunchy toppings will change your sushi experience!

TOOLS & INGREDIENTS

Thanks to the growing popularity of sushi, specialist sushi-making tools and cookware are now much easier to buy. Look in Japanese stores, cookware shops and online.

SUSHI-MAKING TOOLS

Wooden sushi mixing bowl
This is used when mixing rice with sushi vinegar to make sushi rice or adding other ingredients to make mixed rice dishes, such as chirashi sushi. The wood helps to maintain the moisture level of the rice, absorbing any excess moisture. Before using, wet the surface of the bowl to prevent the rice sticking to it. The wide, shallow shape allows the rice to cool quickly and be evenly seasoned. You could use a wide, shallow, glass or ceramic bowl, but avoid using metallic materials which may react with the vinegar.

Bamboo mat
This is the must-have item for your sushi making, especially for creating rolled sushi and egg omelettes. You will also need clingfilm (plastic wrap) for coating the mat, enabling you to roll inside-out rolls. Once you have used the mat, clean the surface and allow to dry thoroughly before storing. If grains of rice have become stuck in the mat, soak the mat in water to soften them and clean it with a fine brush, like a toothbrush. Plastic mats are also available.

Grater
The Japanese grater is designed a little differently to its European version. Instead of holes, it has fine raised spikes which allow the grated ingredient to remain on the surface of the grater. This allows fresh wasabi, ginger, garlic and radish to be turned into a brilliantly fine paste. Once you have tried using this grater, it will become an essential tool in your kitchen.

Peeler
You probably already have a peeler in your kitchen, but Japanese ones are the best. They are used for peeling carrots and asparagus, and also for thinly slicing cucumber and courgette (zucchini) for sushi rolls. There are other variations designed for cutting vegetables into julienne or matchsticks.

Brush
This is used for brushing the sauce on nigiri sushi. Rather than using a spoon or other tools, the brush can give an elegant glaze to the food. A pastry brush made with natural bristles makes a good alternative.

Cooking chopsticks
Using chopsticks for cooking Japanese food is very practical. They can be used for stirring, beating eggs, and so on. They are also useful for serving and adding the garnish toppings to sushi. Cooking chopsticks are much longer than the chopsticks for eating, to protect your hands away from the heat of cooking.

Sashimi knife (yanagiba)
A sharp knife is essential to good sushi. This long, slim knife is used for sashimi, or slicing fish fillets for sushi (see the knife tips on page 13). The blades are carbon steel, so wipe and dry after every use.

Round and square moulds
Used for moulding sushi cakes and sandwiches, and other creative and modern styles of sushi.

Wooden sushi bowl

Round and square moulds

Sashimi knife
(yanagiba)

Grater

Cooking
chopsticks

Bamboo mat

Brush

Peeler

Square egg frying pan (skillet)

Cutters

Fish bone tweezers

Wooden rectangular mould

Square egg frying pan (skillet)

This is designed especially for making the square or rectangular rolled omelette used in sushi tamago (see page 36). In this pan, the egg omelette is made as a thin square omelette and rolled into a long rectangular shape in the pan during the cooking process using cooking chopsticks. Due to this distinctive cooking method, and the constant tilting of the pan during cooking, it is not suitable for use on induction hobs.

Cutters

At first glance these look like cupcake cutters, but they are designed for cutting vegetables (such as carrot and daikon) and are used to stunning effect in Japanese cuisine for toppings or garnishings.

Wooden rectangular mould

Pressed sushi is one of the much-loved classic types of sushi. This mould is for making rectangular sushi or oshi sushi (see page 87) and is perfect for building layers of rice and toppings such as fish or soboro (scrambled egg). The wooden tools for sushi should be soaked in water before use to prevent the rice from sticking, or alternatively line them with clingfilm (plastic wrap).

Fish bone tweezers

If you are preparing fish fillets from scratch, this is a vital little tool for removing bones. After filleting the fish, carefully run your finger over the fillet to detect any remaining bones. Pull out the bone in the direction that it protrudes to avoid damaging the fillet. Even if you buy filleted fish, you may find the odd bone, so this is a very handy tool to have in your kitchen.

KNIFE TIPS

Anyone serious about making sushi or who has started
to prepare sashimi or sushi on a regular basis should buy
a good-quality Japanese sashimi knife, or yanagiba.

I can assure you it is a lifetime investment, and you will be amazed by
what a difference it will make. The yanagiba blade only has a cutting edge
on one side (the other side is flat), so a left-handed knife is also available.
These knives are incredibly sharp, allowing you to slice the fish cleanly and
beautifully thin. The way to use these knives is different from using western
knives. It takes a little practice to get used to it, but once you master it,
it will save you time and money in your sushi preparation.

**To cut across the fibre of the fish, draw the knife towards you in a smooth
motion.** Imagine you are playing the violin, making a beautiful sound by
drawing the bow across its strings - not in a sawing motion! I think the
movement of the knife should be as beautiful as playing the violin.

**If preparing a large fish such as salmon, tuna or yellowtail (hamachi) for
sashimi, place the fish horizontally with the thick side away from you.**
Position the edge of your knife at the edge of the fish and cut across the
fibre of the fish by pressing down gently while drawing the knife towards
you. Use the whole length of the blade from the bottom end to the tip to
slice one fillet.

For slicing lengthways into a long stick (1 x 18 cm/½ x 7 in) for rolls, place
the fillet vertically, angle the tip of the knife at the top of the fish and cut
across the fibre of the fish by drawing the knife towards you.

For skinning the fish, place the fish skin-side down on the chopping board
and insert the knife as close to the skin as possible from the tail end. Cut
about 2-cm/¾-in deep and hold the knife almost parallel to the board.
Pull the skin in the opposite direction to the knife blade, moving the knife
forward to the top of the fish. Use one hand to hold the skin while moving
the knife toward the top of the fish. For the salmon, I like to remove the
brown part of the flesh just under the skin as well.

To care for the knife, always wash in warm water and dry thoroughly after
use. Never put it in a dishwasher. Sharpening with a whetstone is ideal for
Japanese knives.

SASHIMI-QUALITY FISH

It is essential to use only fresh fish when making sashimi and sushi. Talk to your fishmonger to ensure that the fish is fresh in and always ask for sashimi-quality fish, buying the best sashimi-grade fish that is available. Only buy fish on the day you are going to serve it.

It is very important that you yourself go to the fishmonger or fish market to see what is available for your sushi making – you may change your mind about which recipes to cook when you see what is for sale. Needless to say, the freshness of the fish is paramount for sushi- and sashimi-making. Raw fish should always be stored in the refrigerator and eaten within 24 hours of purchase.

The same fish will always differ a little in taste depending on which sea or ocean it has been caught in. In this book I have used salmon, sea bass, mackerel and tuna, all of which are widely available.

There are three kinds of tuna commonly used in sushi and sashimi – bluefin tuna (hon maguro), southern bluefin tuna (minami maguro) and bigeye tuna (mebachi). Tuna is called maguro in Japanese. As it is a big fish, it is usually divided into three categories. Akami is the back part of tuna which is the most familiar lean flesh with an intense ruby colour. Toro is the fatty belly part of tuna, and o-toro is the most prized, expensive part of tuna.

At the fishmonger, you will notice that big fish such as salmon or tuna are usually already prepared and presented in different cuts. The flesh has to be bright in colour and hydrated, but should never be broken or cloudy coloured. If you are not sure about it, always ask the fishmonger if your fillet of choice is of sashimi quality or if it can be eaten raw. He will guide you to the best and freshest fish and give you all the information you need. You will end up learning a lot about the different fish and their qualities through these experiences.

The photograph opposite shows how to cut your fish for the different types of sushi or sashimi you are making. The central part of the fish is not used for sushi as it is too stringy to be eaten raw (use it in cooked dishes instead). See page 13 for information on how to use your sashimi knife.

To check the freshness of a fish and its suitability for use in sushi, there are a few infallible guidelines:

· The eyes should be clear and plump.

· The body should be firm, plump, hydrated and shiny.

· The gills in particular are a great clue for checking for freshness – they should be bright red or pink.

· It is not common practice for customers to touch fish at the fishmonger, but don't hesitate to ask for a closer look at the fish you are interested in buying.

· And last but not least, sniff the fish – if it has an unpleasant smell, you won't want to eat it raw.

Government food safety agencies have issued guidelines for making your own sushi using raw fish, as occasionally raw fish may contain parasitic larvae. If wild fish are to be eaten raw or lightly cooked, ensure that all parts of the fish, especially the thickest parts, have been frozen for at least 4 days in a domestic freezer at -15°C (5°F) or colder. This will ensure that any undetected larvae are killed.

Before freezing, it is best to cut the fish into a block, then wrap in clingfilm (plastic wrap). To defrost, move the frozen fish to the fridge for 5–12 hours before use. Eat on the day of defrosting.

HOW TO CUT FISH

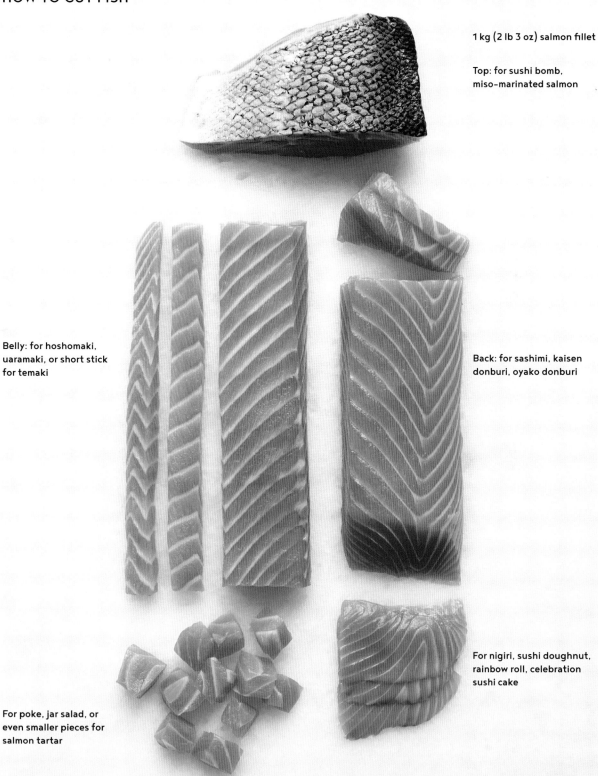

1 kg (2 lb 3 oz) salmon fillet

Top: for sushi bomb,
miso-marinated salmon

Belly: for hoshomaki,
uaramaki, or short stick
for temaki

Back: for sashimi, kaisen
donburi, oyako donburi

For nigiri, sushi doughnut,
rainbow roll, celebration
sushi cake

For poke, jar salad, or
even smaller pieces for
salmon tartar

SEAFOOD

Japan was once said to be the world's biggest consumer of prawns (shrimp), and unsurprisingly they are one of the most popular shellfish when making sushi. Other types of seafood that can be eaten raw include sea urchins, scallops, oysters and squid, all of which make good sushi toppings (always make sure you buy the best quality, suitable for sushi).

PRAWNS (SHRIMP)

There are many varieties of prawns available, from tiny shrimps to large tiger or king prawns (jumbo shrimp). The shells are usually dark grey in colour when raw, changing to pink during cooking. However, some species have pink shells even in their raw state.

If you are tempted to use raw prawns (shrimp) in sushi, always buy from a Japanese fishmonger and ensure you buy the best sashimi-quality. In the recipes that follow, I always use cooked prawns (shrimp).

How to prepare king prawns
This is the method I use for preparing king prawns (jumbo shrimp) for sushi, particularly for the sushi rolls. The prawns are stretched before cooking, and this technique stops the prawns (shrimp) from bending in on themselves during cooking, allowing them to be used for maki and nigiri.

Remove the head of the prawn (shrimp), but keep the shell on. To devein, insert a skewer at the tail, near the back of the prawn (shrimp). Carefully pull out the black vein. This will remove the black intestine without cutting the back of the prawn (shrimp).

Insert a 15-cm (6-in) wooden skewer from the head end along the belly to the tip. Bring a large saucepan of water to the boil. Add the skewered prawns (shrimp) and cook for 2½ minutes, until the flesh turns white and the shells turn pink. Remove the prawns (shrimp) from the pan and dip immediately into a bowl of cold water to stop the cooking process.

When the prawns (shrimp) have cooled, remove from the bowl of water. Remove the skewer by turning it slowly and pulling it gently from the prawn (shrimp). Remove the shells.

To prepare prawns (shrimp) for nigiri, see page 94. For tempura prawns (shrimp), see page 59.

SCALLOPS

Scallops are one of my favourite shellfish. When raw, they have a beautiful sweet flavour and a creamy, silky texture that will melt in your mouth like gelato! To prepare them as sashimi, always purchase hand-dived live scallops in their shells, buying the best sashimi-quality available from specialist fishmongers. Sashimi-quality frozen scallops are also available from Japanese stores.

How to prepare scallops
These are used in the nigiri recipe on page 95. To shell scallops, place the scallop flat side up, with a dish towel underneath to support the shell. Insert an oyster knife at the hinge and carefully open the shell (you could ask your fishmonger to do this for you).

Cut the muscle attached to the flat side of the shell, then use your fingers to separate its frilly skirt and coral from the scallop. Discard the black gut. Use a knife to remove the scallop from the shell. Rinse in cold water, then slice across the fibre.

YOUR SUSHI PANTRY

You may not be so familiar with some of these ingredients, but they are used in many types of sushi. Some are available from supermarkets, but others may need to be sourced from Japanese food stores or online.

Nori
A sheet of roasted seaweed, this is one of the most important ingredients for making rolled sushi. It can also be used for wrapping, bundling, garnishing for other types of sushi or just eaten as a healthy snack. It is high in fibre, protein, vitamins and minerals.

Kombu
This is kelp, an umami-rich dried seaweed that is used not only for making stock, but also for curing fish and vegetables and for flavouring the sushi rice. A quality kombu produced in Hokkaido, northern Japan is widely used in Japanese cuisine.

Dried shiitake
This flavoursome mushroom is believed to have many properties beneficial to health and contains significant quantities of vitamins B and D. Reconstitute before use by soaking in water for at least 30 minutes. You can also use the soaking water as an umami-rich stock (and it is one of the essential ingredients for making a vegetarian/vegan stock).

Rice (Japanese short-grain sushi rice)
Sushi cannot be made without this short-grain, sticky rice. See pages 22–23 for information on how to cook sushi rice.

Black and white sesame seeds
These bring flavour, texture and an accent of colour when used to garnish sushi. Usually, the sesame seeds found in Asian grocery stores have been pre-toasted to enhance the flavours, meaning they can be used straight from the packet without having to dry-roast them. If you use the untoasted ones, put them in a frying pan (skillet), then dry-roast for a minute or so first.

Shiso
The most popular herb in Japan, this is the leaf of the perilla plant. It is used to add an aromatic flavour to sushi and sashimi.

Pickled ginger
Often eaten between different types of sushi as a palate cleanser. Pickled in rice vinegar, it has a mild acidity, ideal for eating after fatty fish.

Ume paste
This paste is made from salted plums and its salty yet tart flavour works well with some fillings for rolls, or toppings. It is also eaten with Japanese rice balls, or Onigiri, Japan's most loved rice ball.

Fresh wasabi rhizome and paste
Wasabi grows in clean streams and is native to Japan, although it is grown in other parts of the world too. Its rhizome is grated and used as a condiment for sushi and sashimi and it has a sharp, characteristic pungent taste. It is also famous for its antibacterial properties. Wasabi leaves and flowers are also edible and available when in season. As it is rare to find fresh wasabi in the supermarket, it is most commonly used in its powdered or paste form.

Nori

Fresh wasabi rhizome and paste

Kombu

Ume paste

Dried shiitake

Black and white
sesame seeds

Pickled ginger

Shiso

Rice (short-grain sushi rice)

White miso

Red miso

Vinegar

Mirin

Light soy sauce

Dark soy sauce

Sake

FIVE FUNDAMENTAL SEASONINGS

When you taste the huge variety of Japanese food, you might not know which seasonings have been used for the dishes. In fact, you can make hundreds of dishes using just these five basic Japanese seasonings.

Soy sauce

Known as shoyu, this Japanese seasoning is used in almost every meal, not just for dipping sushi and sashimi. There are three main kinds of soy sauce. Dark soy sauce is the most common. Light soy sauce preserves the natural colour of ingredients and is a bit saltier than dark. For a wheat-free option, choose tamari, which is the richest in texture and flavour.

Sake

Japan's most celebrated alcoholic drink is made from fermented rice. It is also used in many types of Japanese cooking for making the dish more flavourful - it removes the smell from fish, seafood and meat and also helps flavours penetrate. Cooking sake is also available and it may contain some salt.

Mirin

This is sweetened sake for seasoning many Japanese dishes, such as teriyaki sauce. It gives a delicate sweetness and glazes the surface of the dish.

Rice vinegar

The most important ingredient for sushi rice, it has a mild flavour and pale yellow colour. It's used in ponzu (see page 38) or other sweet and sour dishes.

Miso

Made from fermented soy beans, this is best known for its use in miso soup. White miso has a sweeter taste and is used for marinades. Red has a saltier, aromatic flavour. The darker colour is the result of a longer fermentation. These are several types of smooth miso, and some types that contain grains.

SUSHI VINEGAR

Did you know that the term sushi means 'sour', which is one of the key flavours of sushi rice?

Making your own sushi vinegar is so simple. All you need to do is combine rice vinegar, sugar and salt, but you do need to find a golden ratio of balanced seasonings. If your preference is for a lighter flavoured sushi, try to reduce the sugar and salt, but do taste your vinegar before using as without sweetness, the taste can be a bit too sharp - like a lemonade without any added sugar.

After making sushi vinegar so many times, this is my perfect ratio:

	rice vinegar	sugar	salt
ratio	12 parts	6 parts	1 part

Use fine sugar (such as caster/superfine) and fine salt and measure accurately.

You can make sushi vinegar in advance. To use, add about 10% of the cooked rice volume, e.g. 400 g (4 cups) cooked rice requires 40 ml (3 tablespoons) sushi vinegar.

Note: If you are using another type of vinegar (in case of unavailability of rice vinegar or if experimenting with a new style of sushi), dilute it with water first. Rice vinegar has 4.2–4.5% acidity, whereas the other types, such as wine vinegar or apple cider vinegar, usually have 6% acidity.

SUSHI RICE

The fussiest nations for cooking rice are perhaps Japan and Italy. My husband is Italian and we have the same passion for food, but have a very different philosophy for cooking rice. It has been said that sushi rice represents 60% of the taste of sushi, and this is true! Here is my guide to making it successfully at home.

JAPANESE SHORT-GRAIN RICE

The Japanese staple food is a short, round grain of rice and the main difference to the other types of rice is its stickiness when cooked. Did you know that sticky short-grain rice is more starchy than long- or medium-grain? This means it provides a more stable supply of energy and helps to maintain a healthy blood sugar level.

You can find various brands of special sushi rice in supermarkets, but it is just plain rice suitable for making sushi, to which you add the sushi vinegar (see page 21) after it has been cooked. Rice is grown in many different countries, but I suggest using rice from Japan for the best result.

Rice to water ratio
As a general rule, if you are using rice grown in Japan, use the same quantity of water as rice. Sushi rice grown in other countries tends to be slightly drier, so if using this add 10% more water than rice.

I measure my rice in a measuring cup and use the same cup to measure the water, using 1 cup of rice to 1 cup of water. If using a rice cooker, you will need less water than the amount recommended in the cooker's instruction book; instead, follow my chart.

Calculating rice quantities
In the recipe chapters that follow, the quantity of rice specified is the cooked amount. The chart opposite shows how to work out how much rice to cook. However, don't worry as the precise weight of rice used in the sushi is flexible.

How to cook sushi rice in five easy stages

Wash and drain Wash the rice in cold water until the water becomes clear, then leave to drain in the sieve (strainer) for 30 minutes.

Cook Place the rice and water in a heavy-based saucepan, then cover with a lid (don't remove the lid until the rice has rested). Bring to the boil over a high heat. When the rice starts to boil, turn down to the lowest heat and simmer for the appropriate time according to the amount of rice. See the chart opposite for the amount of water and the relevant cooking time.

Rest When the cooking time is up, remove the pan from the heat, leave the lid on and rest for 10 minutes. All the water should be absorbed by the rice.

Season Wet the surface of the sushi mixing bowl (see page 10) and use a spatula to prevent the rice sticking. Turn the rice into the bowl. Pour the sushi vinegar over the rice and gently use the spatula to cut and mix the rice sideways so that the rice grains aren't broken.

Cool down Cool at room temperature and cover with a damp cloth. Do not put it in the refrigerator for cooling, as this will affect the texture of the rice. The rice should be the same as body temperature - this makes it far easier to mould than cold rice and allows the flavours of the sushi toppings to shine through.

Quantity guide for sushi rice

COOKED WEIGHT	400 g (2½ cups)	800 g (5 cups)	1.2 kg (7½ cups)
uses	4 kinds of rolls, 26 nigiri	4 portions of poke, donburi	celebration cake, mini sushi cakes
TO COOK			
white short-grain rice	180 g (¾ cup)	360 g (1¾ cups)	540 g (2½ cups)
water	200 ml (¾ cup)	400 ml (1¾ cups)	600 ml (2½ cups)
simmering time	9 minutes	12 minutes	15 minutes
TO SEASON			
rice vinegar	2 tablespoons	4 tablespoons	6 tablespoons
sugar	1 tablespoon	2 tablespoons	3 tablespoons
salt	½ teaspoon	1 teaspoon	1½ teaspoons

Using kombu

If you want to use kombu (see page 18) when cooking the rice, place a 5 x 10-cm (2 x 4-in) piece of kombu on top of the rice in the saucepan before cooking. After cooking, discard the kombu.

It's not essential to use kombu, but it does add a delicate taste to the rice and packs it with umami flavour.

Leftover rice

There is a great recipe for using leftover rice on page 125.

When you store leftover sushi rice in the refrigerator, you will find that by the next day it has become hard, but don't waste it! Simply warm it up again by wrapping the rice in clingfilm (plastic wrap) and microwaving on medium for 3 minutes, and the sushi rice will be revived deliciously. You just need to add some extra sushi vinegar to reinstate the sourness.

Leftover rice should be eaten the next day.

SHORT-GRAIN BROWN RICE

Short-grain brown rice is classed as a super food due to its higher fibre and nutritional content, such as vitamin B, protein, gamma-oryzanol, phytic acid and inositol. The last three are less familiar ones but they are known to provide anti-oxidant, anti-carcinogenic and cholesterol-lowering effects. I suggest buying organic whole grains (to avoid digesting any chemicals on the husks).

Try cooking it in a pressure cooker - it will guarantee a better sticky texture and will reduce the cooking time by half. Less water is required if cooking in a pressure cooker.

MAKES 650 G (5 CUPS)
SEASONED BROWN RICE

250 g (1½ cups) brown rice
500 ml (2 cups plus 2 tablespoons) water
(or about 400 ml/1¾ cups if using a pressure cooker)
60 ml (4 tablespoons) sushi vinegar

Wash and soak
Wash the rice, then soak it in a bowl of water for at least 2 hours or overnight in the refrigerator. Drain the rice.

Cook
Place the rice in a heavy-based saucepan with the fresh water. Put the lid on and bring to the boil over a high heat. When the rice starts to boil, reduce to the lowest heat and simmer for the appropriate time according to the amount of rice (usually about 30 minutes, or 15 minutes in a pressure cooker).

Rest and season
Remove the saucepan from the heat, leave the lid on for 10 minutes, then follow the same cooling and seasoning steps for plain sushi rice on page 22.

MULTI-GRAIN WITH SHORT-GRAIN RICE

Enrich and enliven plain rice with mixed grains. You can purchase ready-mixed sachets of these from Japanese supermarkets. The sachets contain anything from five to 16 types of grains, beans and seeds, including rye, black rice, barley and black beans, and more. Each grain makes for a full-flavoured, well-balanced and nutty-textured rice. The unique thing is that the black rice and beans turn the colour of the rice pinkish after you have added sushi vinegar.

To use, simply replace 10-20% of your uncooked rice quantity with the same quantity of grains. Add the multi-grains to your rice before boiling as per the instructions on pages 22-23.

Coloured rice can also be created by tinting the rice a soft pink by rubbing it with pickled beetroot (beet), or turning it a soft shade of green by using matcha powder (see pages 87, 98, 118 and 121). Coloured rice can create a fun, playful look, particularly in the layered sushi cakes on pages 118 and 122.

Top: Short-grain white rice
Middle: Short-grain brown rice
Bottom: Multi-grain rice

CUTTING VEGETABLES

Adding a variety of vegetables to your sushi not only makes it visually appealing, but it is also healthy and gives unique textures to sushi. Some vegetables can be cut in different ways depending on the style of sushi you are making.

Thinly sliced cucumber
Use for rolls and sushi doughnuts. Use a peeler or mandoline to slice the cucumber lengthways as thinly as possible, then remove the seeds or watery part. For the courgette (zucchini) gunkan (see page 73), use a wide peeler in order to keep the width of courgette to wrap around the rice.

Flower-shaped carrot and radish
Use for garnishing chirashi, suko sushi or pickles. Slice rounds of the carrot or radish, then cut out shapes using a Japanese vegetable cutter (see page 12).

Diced or stick-shaped (bell) peppers
Use for jar salads and uramaki spicy tuna rolls. Remove the seeds of peppers and slice them lengthways into 1 cm (½ in) thickness, then cut into cubes if desired.

Red radish three ways
Use for topping of poke, mosaic sushi, kaisen donburi and jar sushi salads. Cut round, very thin slices of radish. Or slice the radish and cut into small cubes. To cut red radish into super-fine sticks, lay some round slices on a chopping board and cut across the rounds very finely. Soak the radishes in water after cutting to remove any bitterness and to stop them drying out. Drain well before serving.

Julienned courgette (zucchini) and carrot
Use for rolls (futomaki, shikai maki) and jar sushi salads. Peel the courgette (zucchini) with a julienne peeler with skin on. For the carrot, peel and then slice.

Sliced avocado
Use for all the inside-out rolls. Cut the avocado in half lengthways and remove the stone/pit, then peel carefully. Slice the avocado lengthways into wedges 1 cm (½ in) thick, then drizzle a teaspoon of freshly squeezed lemon or lime juice over to prevent discolouration.

Avocado domino
Use for topping of inside-out rolls (such as prawn/shrimp tempura). Cut the avocado in half lengthways and remove the stone/pit, then peel carefully. Place the avocado stone-side down on a chopping board, and thinly slice widthways, then press it down and push forwards very carefully so the slices lean in one direction – like dominos! Then stretch the length of the avocado to the same length of the roll (usually 18 cm/7 in). Drizzle a teaspoon of freshly squeezed lemon or lime juice over to prevent discolouration.

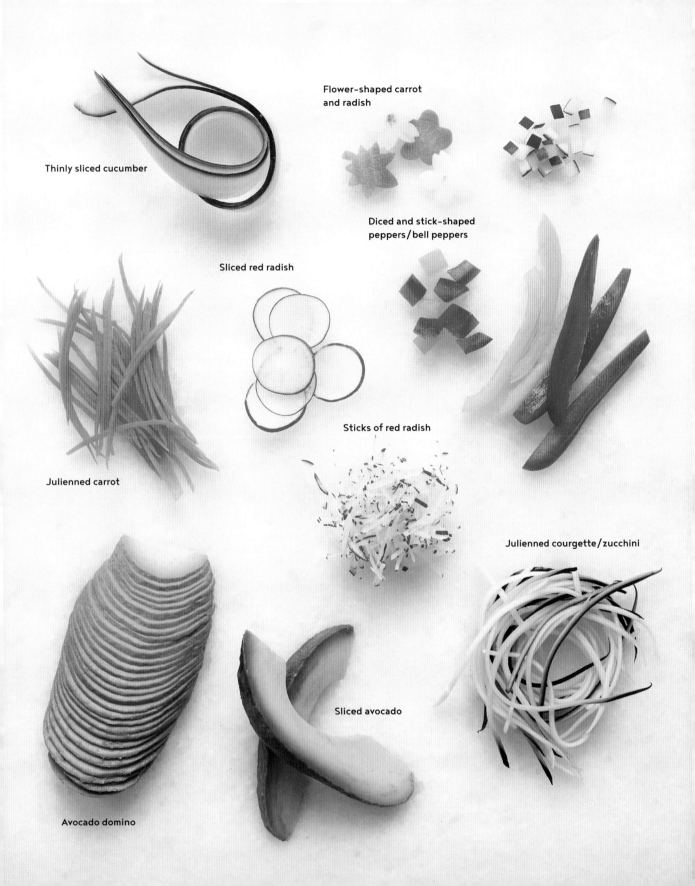

Thinly sliced cucumber

Flower-shaped carrot
and radish

Diced and stick-shaped
peppers/bell peppers

Sliced red radish

Julienned carrot

Sticks of red radish

Julienned courgette/zucchini

Avocado domino

Sliced avocado

NORI

A dried seaweed resembling a sheet of black paper, nori is probably most familiar these days as one of the important ingredients of sushi. Originally nori was not popular outside Japan because it looks like paper, leading to the creation of the best-loved inside-out roll, whose purpose was to hide the nori (see the story behind the spicy tuna roll on page 56).

Quality

My hometown of Saga is located in a region of Japan famous for producing nori of the finest quality, known as Ariake nori. My uncle used to own a nori factory, so my family was always given the best quality nori every season.

There are things to look for in the top grade of nori:

Colour – the richer the colour (like dark purple), the higher the quality. Poor quality nori is often brownish or light green in colour.

Texture – touch the nori. It should be smooth and shiny outside, and make a loud crispy sound when bitten. It should have an even density.

Taste – it should have a rich and deep umami savoury flavour and smell like the ocean.

Nutritional value

An excellent source of fibre, protein, vitamins and minerals, nori is also known to contain a high level of amino acids. It is incredibly healthy and one sheet of nori contains only 3 kcal.

Storing nori

Once opened, nori should be stored with the desiccant in an airtight bag or sealed plastic container in a dark place (but not the fridge as it is vulnerable to humidity so needs to be kept dry). It can be stored in a freezer too.

Cutting nori

Think of nori as paper, and the possibilities of how to use it are endless. You can cut it with scissors or a sharp knife and use it for wrapping for sushi rolls and sushi sandwiches, as well as a crisp garnish with various donburi sushi.

When using it for rolls, cut the nori parallel to the lines on the nori. The lines on the nori sheets are made by the bamboo mats it is roasted on – these can be used as guidelines when cutting the sheets.

Nori has a front and a back – use the shiny side on the outside, and the rough side for sticking to rice.

Sizes of nori
1. Whole sheet 19 x 21 cm (7½ x 8¼ in)
– used for futomaki, chumaki, sushi sandwiches, sushi bomb
2. Half sheet 19 x 10.5 cm (7½ x 4 in)
– used for hosomaki, uramaki, temaki
3. Strips 17 x 3.5 cm (6¾ x 1¼ in)
– used for gunkan
4. Strips 10.5 x 1 cm (4 x ½ in)
– used for nigiri
5. Square 3.5 x 3.5 cm (1¼ x 1¼ in)
– used for nigiri
6. Heart – for showing your love to someone
7. Shredded – chirashi, toppings for donburi-style sushi

BASIC SUSHI TECHNIQUES

These are the basic construction techniques for 'building' the different styles of sushi. You may need to practise a few times to begin with, but it is easy to master the layers and the rolling and folding techniques.

When handing the sushi rice, always dampen your hands with cold water first as this will help to prevent the rice sticking to you. When cutting the sushi rolls, always wipe the blade of the knife with a damp kitchen towel first for a cleaner cut, and re-wipe the blade before each cut.

The number of fillings can vary. For hosomaki rolls, it is usually up to two fillings, while chumaki and futomaki usually have more fillings.

NORI ROLL

1. Place the bamboo mat on the work surface, with the bamboo running horizontally. Place the nori sheet (or half sheet, if specified in the recipe) at the front of the mat with the rough side of the nori face up. Wet your hands with water and spread the rice evenly over the nori, leaving a blank space at the furthest edge of the nori. This space varies in size according to the type of roll - for hosomaki it's 2 cm (¾ in), for futomaki it's 3 cm (1¼ in), for chumaki it's 8 cm (3¼ in). The rice quantity also depends on the type of roll.

2. Make a groove in the middle of the sushi rice using your finger and spread wasabi along the groove if you like it hot. Place the fillings next to each other along the centre.

3. Start rolling! Lift up the edge of the bamboo mat closest to you and roll it away from you.

4. The layers of rice and nori will roll over the filling to enclose it.

5. Keep rolling until the blank edge of the nori furthest from you completes the 'tube'.

6. Unroll the mat, move the sushi roll to a cutting board, then use the mat to create more sushi rolls.

7. Turn the sushi roll so that the join of the nori is on the underside (the nori is dry when rolled, but it absorbs moisture from the rice – placing the seam side down will help to seal the roll). To cut the roll into six pieces, wipe the blade of a knife with a wet kitchen towel – this helps to cut the roll cleanly. Cut across the centre of the roll.

8. Line the two pieces up next to each other. Cut across into three or four pieces, as specified in the recipe. Serve cut-side up to show the fillings in the centre.

URAMAKI

1. Cover a bamboo mat with clingfilm (plastic wrap) to stop the rice sticking to it. Put the mat on a clean, level work surface, then position a sheet of nori (rough side up) at the front of the mat. Wet your hands in water to stop the rice sticking. Take an apple-sized amount of rice and spread it evenly over the nori.

2. Sprinkle toasted sesame seeds over the sushi rice, then carefully turn the nori and rice over together by folding the empty part of the mat over the rice, then flip it over. Open out the mat again and place the rice side closest to you.

3. Lay your chosen fillings down the centre of the nori in neat layers, one on top of another.

4. Start rolling! Fold the near edge of nori over tightly, leaving about 1.5 cm (¾ in) clear at the other end of the nori. Check the fillings in the centre are straight, then press the rice along the mat.

5. Unroll the mat, leaving you with a perfect sushi roll.

6. Wipe a large knife with a wet towel and cut the roll in half across the middle. Place the two halves side by side and cut into four pieces, making eight portions in total.

TEMAKI

1. Cut the nori sheet in half and then hold it flat on your hand, shiny side out. Wet the other hand with water to stop the rice sticking to it. Take an egg-sized handful of sushi rice and gently spread onto one side of the nori. Use your finger to make a groove in the middle of the sushi rice for the fillings.

2. Spread wasabi along the groove, if desired, and then put your favourite fillings on the sushi rice.

3. Now, start rolling! Fold the bottom left corner of the nori over to cover the rice and fillings, folding it up to the top centre of the nori, and creating a cone.

4. Roll the cone to the other end of the nori – it should look like an ice-cream cone. Eat immediately! You will enjoy its crispness at its best just after the nori is rolled. If not eaten immediately, the nori will begin to get soggy.

NIGIRI

1. Wet your hands with water to stop the rice sticking to them. Take a tablespoon of sushi rice and gently shape it in your hands to make a small oval ball. Repeat with your remaining rice.

2. Take a piece of fish about 3 x 7 cm (1¼ x 2¾ in). Place a little wasabi paste onto the piece of fish if you like it hot!

3. Place the rice ball on top of the fish and use your thumb to make an indentation in the centre. This will make for a lighter textured rice.

4. Roll and turn the rice and fish on your fingers, fish-side up, then use the other hand to shape the rice. Push gently from the sides with your thumb and forefinger to stick the rice and fish together, then press the top with your forefinger and middle finger. The fish should cover the rice. Rotate the nigiri to form the shape into an even oblong.

RICE SANDWICHES

1. Line and cover a square mould (8 x 8 cm, 3.5 cm high/ 3¼ x 3¼ in, 1¼ in high) with clingfilm (plastic wrap) to prevent the sushi rice sticking to it. Take a lime-sized amount of rice (about 60 g/ ½ cup) and spread at the bottom, flattening the surface.

2. Place thin slices of cheese on the rice, spread the mustard on, then put the slices of ham on top.

3. Cover with another lime-sized amount of rice (about 60 g/ ½ cup), flattening the surface.

4. Carefully remove the rice sandwich from the mould and place in the centre of nori, at a diagonal angle.

5. Wrap the rice sandwich in the nori by folding each corner into the centre, just like gift wrapping.

6. Continue to fold in the sides of nori until the rice sandwich is completely enclosed. Wrap the sandwiches in clingfilm (plastic wrap), then rest for 10 minutes. Cut the sandwiches diagonally into triangles. Remember to wet the blade of the knife for a clean cut. Leave the clingfilm (plastic wrap) on so that you can pack the sandwich in a bento box.

EGGS THREE WAYS

Although fish often takes centre stage on the sushi scene, the simple egg is actually as important a player! They say if you want to know how good a sushi establishment is, order a tamagoyaki as the training to make tamago comes after mastering fish and rice preparation. But do not let this deter you! The first two recipes are very easy and make wonderful garnishes. The third one needs a bit of practice, but soon you'll be on the road to becoming a great home sushi chef!

KINSHI TAMAGO

Egg ribbons for chirashi sushi, mini sushi cake, suko sushi

2 large (US extra large) eggs
1 teaspoon sugar
a pinch of salt
vegetable oil

1. Break the eggs into a mixing bowl, add the sugar and salt, then mix well.

2. Heat a 24-cm (9½-in) non-stick frying pan (skillet) over a medium heat. Soak a paper towel with a little oil and wipe this around the pan.

3. Pour in a quarter of the egg mixture, tilting the pan to make an even sheet. When the underside has cooked, turn it over to cook the reverse side for a second, then slide onto a plate. Use the paper towel to blot off the excess oil.

3. Repeat to make three more sheets. Cut them in half, then roll up to slice finely.

SOBORO

Egg scrambles for oshi sushi, Christmas sushi, celebration sushi cake

2 large (US extra large) eggs
1 teaspoon sugar
a pinch of salt
vegetable oil

1. Break the eggs into a mixing bowl, add the sugar and salt, then mix well.

2. Heat a small saucepan over a medium heat and add a little oil soaked into the paper towel to wipe off the pan.

3. Pour the egg mixture into the pan and stir using four chopsticks to make fine scrambled egg (or use a whisk).

SUSHI TAMAGO

Egg roll for temaki sushi, mosaic sushi

4 large (US extra large) eggs
1 teaspoon mirin
1 teaspoon light soy sauce
1 tablespoon sugar
a pinch of salt
vegetable oil

MAKES 1 EGG ROLL

1. Break the eggs into a large bowl and crush the egg yolks then cut the egg white using the chopsticks. Mix the other seasonings into the eggs, then stir gently. Heat a square 18 x 18-cm (7 x 7-in) frying pan (skillet) over a high heat and add the oil soaked into the paper towel to wipe off the pan. When the pan is hot enough, pour a quarter of the egg mixture and tilt the pan to spread the mixture. Use chopsticks to break the bubbles on the egg.

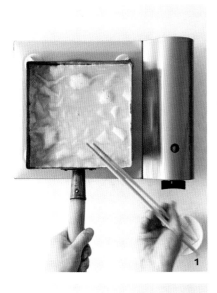

2. When the egg is half cooked, roll the egg towards you.

3. Push the egg roll to the back of the pan. Spread the oil (using the paper towel soaked in the oil) over the pan.

4. Pour in another quarter of the egg mixture, tilting the pan slightly so that the new mixture spreads under the first egg roll. When the mixture is half cooked, roll the first egg roll over the new egg to form a fatter roll.

5. Repeat another two times to use up the remaining egg mixture. After the last roll, turn the heat off.

6. Put the bamboo mat on a chopping board and transfer the egg roll on to it. Wrap the egg roll in the bamboo mat and leave it to rest for 3 minutes. Unroll the bamboo mat, remove the egg roll and slice into eight pieces for nibbles, ten pieces for nigiri, or cut it lengthways for rolls.

SOY-BASED SAUCES

Soy sauce is not only beautiful as it is, but its versatile aromatic flavour works perfectly with other seasonings or condiments. Here are some variations of my classic sauces for your everyday salad, sashimi and sushi.

TERIYAKI SAUCE

3 tablespoons shoyu (Japanese dark soy sauce)
3 tablespoons sake
3 tablespoons mirin
1 tablespoon brown sugar

Bring all the ingredients to the boil in a small saucepan and stir well until the brown sugar has dissolved and the alcohol has evaporated. To make it thicker, simmer over a low heat for a couple of minutes. Store in the fridge for a couple of weeks.

KABAYAKI SAUCE

3 tablespoons shoyu (Japanese dark soy sauce)
3½ tablespoons mirin
2 tablespoons water (or dashi stock)
½ tablespoon katakuriko (potato starch), mixed with 1 tablespoon cold water

Bring the shoyu, mirin and water (or dashi stock) to the boil in a saucepan, reduce the heat to low, then pour the katakuriko and water mixture in slowly to thicken the sauce. Store in the fridge for a week.

SOY SESAME DRESSING

1 tablespoon toasted sesame oil
2 tablespoons vegetable oil
2 garlic cloves, thinly sliced
2 teaspoons finely chopped ginger
1 dried chilli, if you like it hot
3 tablespoons shoyu (Japanese dark soy sauce)
2 tablespoons mirin
2 tablespoons toasted white sesame seeds

Place the sesame oil and vegetable oil in a saucepan over a medium heat. When they become hot (but not at high smoking point), add the garlic and fry until a light golden colour, but be careful not to burn the garlic.

Turn the heat off and remove the garlic chips from the pan. Drain the garlic on a paper towel and use as a topping for your dish.

Add the ginger and dried chilli (if using) to the pan while the oil is still hot. It may sizzle and the residual heat will cook them.

When the oil has cooled, add the shoyu, mirin and sesame seeds. Store in the fridge for a couple of weeks.

SIMPLE PONZU SAUCE

3½ tablespoons rice vinegar
3½ tablespoons mirin
3½ tablespoons shoyu (Japanese dark soy sauce)
2 tablespoons lime juice

Combine all the ingredients in a jar. Store in the fridge for up to three days.

WASABI + SOY SAUCE

This goes well with most nigiri sushi. Rather than dissolving wasabi in soy sauce, top your sushi with a little wasabi paste, then dip in soy sauce.

YUZU KOSHO + SOY SAUCE

This green chilli pepper paste mixed with yuzu citrus zest is a famous product from my hometown. Mix equal quantities of each. My family always had a homemade one in the fridge and used it for hotpot dishes, grilled seafood and sashimi.

Top left: Yuzu kosho and soy sauce
Top right: Teriyaki sauce
Middle left: Wasabi and soy sauce
Middle right: Soy sesame dressing
Bottom left: Kabayaki sauce
Bottom right: Simple ponzu sauce

CREAMY SAUCES

These sauces can be made in advance and stored in the fridge. Their thick and creamy texture means they can be used in rolls and for topping sushi. Alternatively, use them as dips and serve with vegetable sticks.

SESAME DRESSING

3 tablespoons sesame paste (light tahini)
3 tablespoons usukuchi shoyu (light soy sauce)
3 tablespoons mirin
1½ tablespoons rice vinegar
1 tablespoon saikyo miso (white sweet smooth miso)
1 garlic clove, grated
1 shallot, finely chopped
black sesame seeds, to garnish

Mix the sesame paste with the light soy sauce until smooth, then add the mirin and stir until well combined. Add the remaining ingredients to make a smooth dressing (if you wish, use a hand mixer or food processor). Sprinkle over the black sesame seeds before serving. Store in the fridge for a couple of weeks. This is used in the jar salad on page 144.

MISO DENGAKU

2 tablespoons red miso (smooth texture)
1 tablespoon agave
½ tablespoon mirin
½ tablespoon sake
1 tablespoon water

Combine all the ingredients in a small saucepan, then simmer over a low heat, stirring, for 1 minute. Allow to cool. Store in the fridge for a couple of weeks.

This sauce is used in vegetable sushi, especially for aubergine (eggplant) which is commonly served with miso dengaku.

MAYONNAISE-BASED SAUCES

These spicy, creamy mayonnaise-based sauces add a delicious accent to your sushi (either use them inside your sushi or as a dipping sauce). Personally I prefer the spice not to overwhelm the other flavours, but I know that others have different tastes. As everyone has their own preferences, all you need to know is the spiciness of each condiment and find the perfect balance to suit you. Below are my well-balanced ratios of spicy sauces.

	ratios	
spicy mayo	3 parts mayonnaise	1 part sriracha sauce
spicy yuzu mayo	9 parts mayonnaise	1 part yuzu kosho paste
wasabi mayo	5 parts mayonnaise	1 part wasabi paste

Top: Sesame dressing
Middle: Miso dengaku
Bottom left: Spicy yuzu mayonnaise
Bottom right: Spicy mayonnaise

巻き寿司
SUSHI ROLLS

HOSOMAKI
PICKLED PEPPERS / CUCUMBER UME

These stylish vegetarian hosomaki are a modern and healthy way to enjoy classic
rolled sushi. I have made these with two different fillings – the gorgeous colours
of the pickled peppers will whet your appetite, while the cucumber filling has
a dash of ume for tangy flavour. Cut the rolls diagonally to show off the fillings!

PICKLED PEPPERS

MAKES 4 ROLLS

2 sheets of nori, cut in half
300 g (2 cups) seasoned
  multi-grain sushi rice (cooked
  weight, see pages 22-24)
wasabi
soy sauce, to serve

FOR THE PICKLED PEPPERS
½ red (bell) pepper
½ yellow (bell) pepper
1 tablespoon rice bran oil
4 tablespoons mirin
4 tablespoons rice vinegar
zest of 1 orange
1 garlic clove, sliced
a pinch of salt

1. To make pepper pickles, preheat the grill (broiler)
to high or the oven to 200°C/400°F/Gas 6. Cut
the peppers into quarters, remove the seeds and
lightly oil the skin. Place the peppers skin-side up
on a baking sheet, and grill (broil) on high for about
12 minutes until the skin blisters. Wrap the peppers
in foil so that the steam softens the skin. When the
peppers have cooled, peel the skins off.

2. Mix the other pickle ingredients together in a bowl,
add the skinned peppers and marinate for at least
20 minutes or overnight.

3. Remove the peppers from the bowl and cut into
long strips. (Note: this recipe only uses a quarter of
the pickled peppers, but the remainder can be stored
in the fridge for a week or used in other recipes.)

4. Make the hosomaki rolls following the instructions
on pages 30-31, spreading the wasabi and pickled
peppers in the groove in the rice .

CUCUMBER UME

MAKES 4 ROLLS

2 sheets of nori, cut in half
300 g (2 cups) seasoned sushi rice
  (cooked weight, see pages 22-23)
1 tablespoon ume paste
4 cucumber sticks, cut into sticks
  1 x 18 cm (½ x 7 in)
soy sauce, to serve
wasabi, to serve

1. Make the cucumber hosomaki rolls following the
instructions on pages 30-31, spreading the ume
paste and cucumber sticks in the groove in the rice.

2. Serve with soy sauce and wasabi.

HOSOMAKI
SALMON AND CHIVE / SMOKED MACKEREL

Hosomaki literally means 'thin roll' and this describes very accurately what it is! It usually has only one or two fillings as there's not really much space for more, but this simplicity requires precision. Salmon and chive is one of the simplest fillings, but it is a classic and popular combination. Smoked mackerel is one of my favourite ingredients and it goes so well with English mustard. The smoky and salty flavours complement the nutty brown sushi rice, and the little kick of mustard makes a good alternative to wasabi.

SALMON AND CHIVE

MAKES 4 ROLLS

100 g (3½ oz) sashimi-quality salmon
5 g (¼ oz) chives
2 sheets of nori, cut in half
300 g (2 cups) seasoned sushi rice (cooked weight, see pages 22–23)
soy sauce, to serve

1. Cut the salmon into sticks 1 cm (½ in) thick and 18 cm (7 in) long.

2. Make the salmon and chive hosomaki rolls following the instructions on pages 30–31, adding the chives and salmon sticks to the groove in the rice.

3. To cut each roll into six pieces, wipe a knife with a wet towel (see page 31). Cut across the centre of one roll, then line up the two pieces side by side. Cut across into three pieces. Repeat with the remaining rolls, and serve to show the fillings in the centre.

SMOKED MACKEREL

MAKES 4 ROLLS

1 fillet of smoked mackerel
¼ cucumber
2 sheets of nori, cut in half
300 g (2 cups) seasoned brown sushi rice (cooked weight, see pages 22–24)
1 teaspoon English mustard
soy sauce, to serve

1. Remove the bones from the mackerel fillet using tweezers (see page 12), then cut into four long strips.

2. Cut the cucumber into long, thin strips.

3. Make the hosomaki rolls following the instructions on pages 30–31 and spreading a little mustard along the groove in the rice.

4. To cut each roll into six pieces, wipe a knife with a wet towel (see page 31). Cut across the centre of one roll, then line up the two pieces side by side. Cut across into three pieces. Repeat with the remaining rolls, and serve to show the fillings in the centre.

CHUMAKI
PRAWN AND AVOCADO

Chumaki are medium-sized rolls and are arguably the easiest sushi rolls to make as they are just 'the right size'! Usually made with two or three fillings, they also differ from the hosomaki featured on the previous pages as they each use a whole sheet of nori and twice the quantity of rice. This recipe uses a favourite combination of prawn (shrimp) and avocado as the filling – always a winner!

MAKES 4 ROLLS

½ avocado
1 teaspoon freshly squeezed
   lemon juice
4 sheets of nori
600 g (4 cups) seasoned
   sushi rice (cooked weight,
   see pages 22–23)
160 g (5½ oz) cooked king prawns
   (jumbo shrimp), shelled
   (see page 17)
soy sauce, to serve

1. Slice the avocado lengthways into eight pieces. Sprinkle with the lemon juice to prevent the flesh turning brown.

2. Make the chumaki rolls following the instructions on pages 30–31, spreading the avocado slices and the prawns (shrimp) in the groove in the rice.

3. To cut each roll into eight pieces, wipe a knife with a wet towel (see page 31). Cut across the centre of one roll, then line up the two pieces side by side. Cut across into four pieces. Repeat with the remaining rolls, and serve cut-side up to show the fillings in the centre.

CHUMAKI

SMOKED SALMON AND CREAM CHEESE

This roll is inspired by the South American sushi I tried in Argentina. I was completely shocked when I saw 'raw salmon with cream cheese' on the menu in a restaurant in Buenos Aires, as I couldn't believe that sushi would work with a cheese filling. But it does, especially when partnered with salmon! I have created this smoked salmon, rocket (arugula) and cream cheese recipe for you to try as this is a familiar combination of ingredients in western cookery and you know it is delicious. Using multi-grain rice adds a pretty colour element to this sushi, rather like the colours of cherry blossom in the spring!

MAKES 4 ROLLS

4 sheets of nori
**600 g (4 cups) seasoned
  multi-grain sushi rice (cooked
  weight, see pages 22-24)**
120 g (4 oz) cream cheese
**120 g (4 oz) smoked salmon,
  cut into strips**
**a handful of wild rocket
  (arugula) leaves**
soy sauce, to serve

1. Make the chumaki rolls following the instructions on pages 30-31, carefully spreading the cream cheese in the groove in the rice, then topping with the smoked salmon slices and rocket (arugula) leaves.

2. To cut each roll into eight pieces, wipe a knife with a wet towel (see page 31). Cut across the centre of one roll, then line up the two pieces side by side. Cut across into four pieces. Repeat with the remaining rolls, and serve cut-side up to show the fillings in the centre.

FUTOMAKI
SPICY TUNA, SPINACH AND EGG ROLL

Futomaki are 'thick rolls', containing four or five fillings, with the choice of ingredients all balanced to create the perfect balance of colour, flavour and texture. Futomaki are slightly harder to make than the previous rolls in this chapter due to the increased number of fillings. Unlike a classic filling, I made a spicy version with Korean red chilli miso to season the tuna. Because it is a big roll, you can enjoy a different taste in every bite! Make sure you keep all the ingredients in place so they don't smear into each other. You want to cut into the roll and discover a beautiful mosaic of fillings and enjoy a harmony of flavours and textures!

MAKES 2 ROLLS

60 g (2½ oz) can of tuna in oil
1 garlic clove, chopped
1 tablespoon mirin
½ tablespoon gochujang miso
   (Korean red chilli miso)
½ carrot, cut into fine matchsticks
   (see page 26)
60 g (1 cup) fresh spinach
2 sheets of nori
500 g (3 cups) seasoned sushi
   rice (cooked weight, see
   pages 22-23)
2 long strips of egg roll, 18 x 2 cm
   (7 x ¾ in) (see pages 36-37)
2 long sticks of cucumber, 18 x 1 cm
   (7 x ½ in)

1. To make spicy tuna filling, drain the oil from the can into a small frying pan (skillet). Heat the oil over a medium heat, add the tuna, garlic, mirin and gochujang miso and fry, stirring constantly, until the liquid has evaporated. Set aside to cool.

2. Blanch the carrot matchsticks for 1-2 minutes. Also blanch the spinach for a minute, then soak in a bowl of cold water to stop the cooking process. Drain well and squeeze the spinach to get rid of all the water.

3. Make the futomaki rolls following the instructions on pages 30-31, layering the filling in the groove in the rice. Begin with the largest filling, such as the egg roll, followed by the remaining fillings.

4. Wipe a knife with a wet towel (see page 31) and cut each roll into eight pieces. Serve to show the fillings in the centre.

URAMAKI
TUNA MAYO AND PICKLED BEETROOT

This is an anglicized uramaki using some of the most loved sandwich fillings. Not only do they taste great in a roll, but the contrasting colours really stand out when you cut the roll and present each piece cut-side up. If you are not familiar with using raw fish, then this is the perfect sushi recipe for you to start with as it uses canned tuna (the recipe overleaf also combines tuna and avocado in an uramaki roll, but in that instance the tuna is fresh). This is a fantastic combination of fillings and ideal for your lunchbox.

MAKES 4 ROLLS

400 g (2½ cups) seasoned sushi rice (cooked weight, see pages 22–23)
2 sheets of nori, cut in half

FILLINGS
80 g (3 oz) can of tuna, drained
2 tablespoons mayonnaise
½ avocado
1 teaspoon freshly squeezed lemon juice
4 pickled beetroots (beets), cut into thin sticks

TOPPINGS
2 teaspoons toasted black sesame seeds
2 teaspoons toasted white sesame seeds
fronds from 4 sprigs of dill

1. Mix the tuna with the mayonnaise.

2. Slice the avocado lengthways into eight pieces. Sprinkle with the lemon juice to prevent the flesh turning brown.

3. Make the uramaki rolls following the instructions on page 32. Sprinkle the toasted sesame seeds over the sushi rice, and place the dill fronds on the rice, then carefully turn the nori and rice over so the nori is uppermost.

4. Spread the avocado slices and the other filling ingredients along the rice.

5. To cut each roll into eight pieces, wipe a knife with a wet towel (see page 31). Cut across the centre of one roll, then line up the two pieces side by side. Cut across into two pieces. Repeat with the remaining rolls, and serve cut-side up to show the fillings in the centre.

URAMAKI
SPICY TUNA CALIFORNIA ROLL

Not the most traditional but certainly one of the most popular kind of sushi, California Rolls are said to have been created in Los Angeles in the 1960s by a clever Japanese chef. Observing that his customers were turned off by the look of the nori seaweed wrapping, he decided to create inside-out rolls (uramaki) and replaced fatty tuna (toro) with avocado, an ingredient never used before in sushi making! This recipe is the most popular inside-out roll in my sushi-making class. I use both tuna and avocado for a balance in colour and for maximum creaminess, and for a little extra kick, my own spicy mayo sauce.

MAKES 4 ROLLS

400 g (2½ cups) seasoned sushi rice (cooked weight, see pages 22-23)
2 sheets of nori, cut in half

FILLINGS
½ avocado
1 teaspoon freshly squeezed lemon juice
4 tablespoons spicy mayo (see page 41)
100 g (3½ oz) sashimi-quality tuna, diced
4 long, thin slices of cucumber, 1 x 18 cm (½ x 7 in)
¼ red (bell) pepper, cut into fine sticks

TOPPINGS
2 teaspoons toasted black sesame seeds
2 teaspoons toasted white sesame seeds
fronds from 4 sprigs of dill
20 g (¾ oz) yuzu-flavoured tobiko (flying fish roe)

1. Slice the avocado lengthways into eight pieces. Sprinkle with the lemon juice to prevent the flesh turning brown.

2. Make the uramaki rolls following the instructions on page 32. Sprinkle the toasted sesame seeds over the sushi rice, and place the dill fronds on the rice, then carefully turn the nori and rice over so the nori is uppermost.

3. Spread the spicy mayo over the nori, then arrange the cucumber, avocado, red (bell) pepper and tuna on the rice.

4. To cut each roll into eight pieces, wipe a knife with a wet towel (see page 31). Cut across the centre of one roll, then line up the two pieces side by side. Cut across into four pieces. Repeat with the remaining rolls. Serve cut-side up to show the fillings in the centre and sprinkle over the tobiko.

URAMAKI

PRAWN TEMPURA WITH CORIANDER

Everything is right about this recipe from the perfect balance of textures between the softness of the avocado and the crunchiness of the prawn (shrimp), to the ideal balance of taste with the oiliness of the tempura and the freshness of the coriander (cilantro) and zesty sweet chilli sauce.

MAKES 4 ROLLS

400 g (2½ cups) seasoned sushi rice (cooked weight, see pages 22–23)
2 sheets of nori, cut into half
sweet chilli sauce with a squeeze of lime juice, for dipping

FILLINGS
8 king prawn tempura (see below)
½ avocado, cut lengthways into 8 slices
1 teaspoon freshly squeezed lime juice
5 g (¼ cup) coriander (cilantro) leaves

TOPPING
2 avocados, cut in domino style (see page 26)
1 tablespoon freshly squeezed lime juice

PRAWN TEMPURA
8 raw king prawns (jumbo shrimp), shelled, deveined, tail on
1 large (US extra large) egg yolk
75 ml (5 tablespoons) iced water (put ice cubes in water to cool it down)
30 g (scant 4 tablespoons) plain (all-purpose) flour
20 g (2¼ tablespoons) rice flour
vegetable oil, for deep frying

1. To trim the prawns (shrimp), score the belly widthways, then pound it lightly with the flat blade of the knife to stretch the back of the prawns.

2. Mix the egg yolk and iced water in a medium mixing bowl. Combine the two flours in a separate bowl, then add to the water and egg yolk mixture. Slowly mix the batter with chopsticks or a spoon. Don't worry if it looks lumpy – the key to crisp tempura is not to overmix the batter.

3. Heat the oil in a large frying pan (skillet). Drop a little batter into the oil to test if the temperature is between 170–180°C (340–360°F) – the batter should rise to the surface, sizzling, with a couple of seconds.

4. Dip each prawn (shrimp) into the batter and hold over the bowl to drain off any excess. Deep fry a couple of prawns (shrimp) at a time (overcrowding the pan will cause the temperature to drop). Control the heat between medium to high to keep the temperature correct.

5. Turn them over a few times until they are crisp – this should take 2–3 minutes. Drain any excess oil on paper towels.

6. To slice the avocado, see page 26. Squeeze the lime juice over the avocado, then cover with clingfilm (plastic wrap).

7. Make the uramaki rolls following the instructions on page 32, but without any sesame seed toppings. Unroll the mat, place the sliced avocado on top of the roll, gently cover with the bamboo mat, then press to stick the avocado to the roll. Cover the surface of roll with the clingfilm (plastic wrap) to support the avocado and roll together.

8. To cut each roll into eight pieces, wipe a knife with a wet towel (see page 31). Cut across the centre of one roll, then cut each half into four pieces and remove the clingfilm (plastic wrap). Serve with sweet chilli sauce and lime juice.

URAMAKI
RAINBOW ROLLS

This roll is a true showstopper and surprisingly easy to make. At first, it's the wonderful combination of colours and fish that entice, but after one bite, it's the beautiful marriage of salmon and avocado that will keep your tastebuds longing for more. Here I presented the sushi on wasabi leaves for a stark contrast of colours, but you can easily replace them with nasturtium leaves or even lettuce leaves.

MAKES 4 ROLLS

400 g (2½ cups) seasoned sushi rice (cooked weight, see pages 22–23)
2 sheets of nori, cut in half
soy sauce, to serve

FILLINGS
½ avocado
1 teaspoon freshly squeezed lemon juice
100 g (3½ oz) sashimi-quality salmon, cut into 18-cm (7-in) strips

TOPPINGS
160 g (6 oz) sashimi-quality salmon, thinly sliced
80 g (3 oz) sashimi-quality sea bass, thinly sliced
8 sushi prawns (shrimp) (see prawn nigiri, page 94)
½ avocado, thinly sliced
1 teaspoon freshly squeezed lemon juice
4 red radishes, thinly sliced
80 g (3 oz) ikura (salmon roe)
2 tablespoons spicy yuzu mayonnaise (see page 41)

1. Slice the avocado for the filling lengthways into eight pieces. Sprinkle with the lemon juice to prevent the flesh turning brown. Prepare the avocado for the topping in the same way.

2. Make the four uramaki rolls following the instructions on page 32, placing the salmon and avocado alongside each other.

3. Unroll the mat, then top the roll with the salmon, sea bass, prawns (shrimp) and avocado slices, laying them diagonally across the roll.

4. To cut the roll carefully, cover the surface of roll with clingfilm (plastic wrap) to hold the toppings in place.

5. To cut each roll into eight pieces, wipe a knife with a wet towel (see page 31). Cut across the centre of one roll, then cut each half into four pieces and remove the clingfilm (plastic wrap).

6. Garnish with slices of red radish topped with salmon roe (keep the radish in place with a dab of spicy yuzu mayo).

URAMAKI
ITALIAN ROLLS

Being married to an Italian means I always keep Italian staples in my pantry. This uramaki recipe was created one Sunday morning when I wanted to make something quick and simple with what we had in the fridge, and it turned out to be a hit in our international household! It goes to show that with a little imagination and a good understanding of ingredients, you can make something delicious without making a special trip to the shops.

MAKES 4 ROLLS

2 teaspoons balsamic vinegar
400 g (2½ cups) seasoned sushi rice (cooked weight, see pages 22–23)
2 sheets of nori, cut into half

PESTO
a handful of basil leaves, chopped (save the baby leaves for garnishing)
1 garlic clove, chopped
2 tablespoons extra virgin olive oil
a pinch of salt

FILLINGS
4 asparagus spears, trimmed
a little olive oil, for frying
100 g (3 oz) mozzarella cheese, cut into long sticks 1 cm (½ in) thick
16 semi-sundried tomatoes, diced

TOPPINGS
80 g (3½ oz) Parma ham
4 figs, cut into thin wedges
shavings of Parmesan cheese
a few small basil leaves

1. First prepare the balsamic vinegar rice by adding the balsamic vinegar to the seasoned sushi rice, then mix to combine well.

2. To make the pesto, chop the basil leaves then add to a pestle and mortar with the chopped garlic. Pound into a paste (or chop them finely on chopping board). Add the olive oil and season with a pinch of salt, and mix together.

3. Heat a medium frying pan (skillet), add a little olive oil then fry (or grill/broil) the asparagus for 2–3 minutes until lightly browned. Wipe off any excess oil on the asparagus.

4. Make the uramaki rolls following the instructions on page 32, laying down the mozzarella, spreading pesto, and then adding the asparagus and semi-sundried tomatoes down the centre of the nori in neat layers.

5. Unroll the bamboo mat, then place the Parma ham on top of the rice and press gently with the bamboo mat to hold it in place.

6. To cut each roll into eight pieces, wipe a knife with a wet towel (see page 31). Cut across the centre of one roll, then line up the two pieces side by side. Cut across into four pieces.

7. Drizzle each piece with a little pesto and top with fig wedges, Parmesan shavings and basil leaves.

TEMAKI PARTY

Why not throw a make-your-own-sushi party for your friends? In Japan, hand-rolled sushi is the most popular style of sushi at gatherings of family and friends. It is so easy to host a temaki party - simply prepare the sushi rice and cut the fillings into sticks, and that's it! Your guests can then take over, rolling the rice and fillings in a crispy sheet of nori into an ice-cream cone shape. Temakeria are popular in South America where you can order fillings and toppings for freshly made temaki - it's like a sushi version of a gelateria! Here I have supplied three different fillings for your sushi party - my version of a refreshing Latin American crab meat temaki with spicy salsa, a beef and watercress temaki, and a fish temaki using salmon and tuna. These combined quantities will feed four people.

MEXICAN TEMAKI

MAKES 4 ROLLS

120 g (¾ cup) seasoned sushi rice (cooked weight, see pages 22–23)
2 sheets of nori, cut in half

FILLINGS
80 g (3 oz) mixed white and brown crab meat
¼ avocado, sliced
1 teaspoon freshly squeezed lemon juice
4 lettuce leaves, shredded

MEXICAN SALSA
1 tomato, chopped
¼ red onion, chopped
2 tablespoons chopped coriander (cilantro)
½ teaspoon freshly squeezed lime juice
½ tablespoon rice vinegar
¼ teaspoon sugar
a few drops of green tabasco (mild or hot, as you prefer)
1 red jalapeño (chile) pepper, sliced
sea salt, to season

1. To make the Mexican salsa, combine all the ingredients in a bowl, then set aside.

2. Just before serving, slice the avocado and sprinkle with lemon juice to prevent it going brown.

3. To make the cones of sushi, see the instructions on page 33. Add a spoonful of the salsa to the crab meat, avocado and lettuce fillings.

4. Eat immediately! The nori will be at its crispy best just after rolling. If not eaten immediately, the nori will become soggy.

BEEF TEMAKI

MAKES 4 ROLLS

120 g (¾ cup) seasoned sushi rice
  (cooked weight, see pages 22–23)
2 sheets of nori, cut in half
wasabi paste, to serve
soy sauce, to serve

FILLINGS
80 g (3 oz) beef steak
  (sirloin or rib eye)
vegetable oil
small bunch of watercress
salt and freshly ground black
  pepper

1. To fry the beef, rub the steak in vegetable oil, then season with salt and pepper. Heat a frying pan (skillet) to hot, then fry the steak for 1½ minutes on each side for medium rare. Allow the steak to rest, covered with foil, for 2–3 minutes, then slice into strips 1 cm (½ in) thick.

2. To make the cones of sushi, see the instructions on page 33. Add a piece of beef and other fillings of your choice.

3. Eat immediately! The nori will be at its crispy best just after rolling. If not eaten immediately, the nori will become soggy.

FISH TEMAKI

MAKES 20 ROLLS

600 g (4 cups) seasoned sushi rice
  (cooked weight, see pages 22–23)
10 sheets of nori, cut in half
wasabi paste, to serve
soy sauce, to serve

FILLINGS
300 g (10 oz) selection of sashimi-
  quality fish (such as salmon,
  medium fatty tuna and tuna)
1 sushi omelette (see pages 36–37)
1 ripe avocado
1 teaspoon freshly squeezed
  lemon juice
1 red or orange (bell) pepper, sliced
⅓ cucumber, cut into 7-cm (2¾-in)
  sticks
5 whole shiso leaves
pickled ginger

1. Slice the fish into sticks 1 x 6 cm (½ x 2½ in) (see page 13).

2. Make the sushi omelette (see pages 36–37) and slice into pieces the same size as the fish.

3. Just before serving, slice the avocado lengthways and sprinkle with lemon juice to prevent it going brown.

4. To make the cones of sushi, see the instructions on page 33. Add a piece of fish and other fillings of your choice.

5. Eat immediately! The nori will be at its crispy best just after rolling. If not eaten immediately, the nori will become soggy.

GUNKAN MAKI
NORI-WRAPPED RICE TOPPED WITH SALMON AND EGG YOLK

The French will tell you that tartare tastes better served with an egg yolk! So for my Japanese sushi version of French salmon tartare, I topped the salmon with a quail's egg yolk for extra creaminess, plus a little bit of yuzu kosho (Japanese citrusy chilli paste) to shake things up. Alternatively, you can go French-style if you can't find any yuzu kosho and use Tabasco and chopped gherkins (pickles) instead.

MAKES 24

4 sheets of nori
360 g (2¼ cups) seasoned sushi rice (cooked weight, see pages 22–23)
soy sauce, to serve

TOPPINGS
300 g (10 oz) sashimi-quality salmon, finely chopped
1 shallot, finely chopped, soaked in water to remove bitterness
2 tablespoons capers in salted water, drained and finely chopped
a pinch of salt
1 tablespoon finely chopped coriander (cilantro) leaves
¼ teaspoon yuzu kosho (optional)
24 quail's egg yolks
10-cm (4-in) piece of cucumber, thinly sliced into half-moons

1. Cut each sheet of nori into six long strips, each 3.5 x 17 cm (1½ x 6¾ in). You will need 24 strips in total.

2. To make the salmon tartare, mix the salmon, drained shallot, capers, salt, coriander (cilantro) and yuzu kosho, if using, in a bowl.

3. Wet your hand in water to stop the rice sticking to it. Take a tablespoon (15 g/½ oz) of sushi rice and gently shape it into an oval ball. Repeat to make 24 balls. Set aside.

4. Wrap each rice ball with a nori strip. Close the end with a grain of rice to seal.

5. Just before serving, carefully break the quail's eggs to separate the yolks from the whites.

6. Top each rice parcel with some salmon tartare and two pieces of cucumber, then carefully place a yolk on top.

7. Serve them immediately with soy sauce. The nori will become soggy if left for too long.

GUNKAN MAKI
NORI-WRAPPED RICE TOPPED WITH SALMON ROE

Gunkan maki take their name from their shape, with 'gunkan' meaning 'battleship'. These balls of sushi rice wrapped with nori are traditionally topped with fish roe, such as salmon roe (ikura) and sea urchin (uni). You instantly forget the military connotation of the name once the sweetness and the umami of the fish roe hit your tastebuds. For this recipe, I have marinated the salmon roe to restore the eggs' plumpness and reduce the saltiness.

MAKES 24

360 g (2¼ cups) seasoned sushi rice (cooked weight, see pages 22-23)
4 sheets of nori
wasabi paste (optional)
soy sauce, to serve

MARINADE
100 ml (scant ½ cup) dashi
2 tablespoons mirin
2 teaspoons light soy sauce

TOPPING
200 g (7 oz) salmon roe

1. To make the marinade, place the dashi and mirin in a small saucepan. Bring to the boil for 30 seconds to evaporate any alcohol, then remove from the heat and allow to cool. Add the light soy sauce to the mixture, then chill in the refrigerator.

2. Once the marinade is chilled, add the salmon roe and marinade in the fridge for a couple of hours. Drain the seasonings.

3. Cut each sheet of nori into six long strips, each 3.5 x 17 cm (1½ x 6¾ in). You will need 24 strips in total.

4. Wet your hand in water to stop the rice sticking to it. Take a tablespoon (15 g/ ½ oz) of sushi rice and gently shape it into an oval ball. Repeat to make 24 balls. Set aside.

5. Wrap each rice ball with a nori strip. Close the end with a grain of rice to seal.

6. Place the wasabi on the rice and top with the salmon roe.

7. Serve them immediately with soy sauce. The nori will become soggy if left for too long.

GUNKAN MAKI
COURGETTE-WRAPPED RICE TOPPED WITH CRAB MEAT

This is my new version of a gunkan recipe. I was so pleased to come up with this idea of replacing the nori with a ribbon of courgette (zucchini) which bends to make a perfect gunkan shape! I love the mixture of white and brown crab meat which brings a creamy texture and complexity of deep bitter flavour. To add a crunchiness for the topping, I added the apple and red radish. This recipe works well as a canapé as the courgette (zucchini) does not become soggy, as nori would.

MAKES 24

2 courgettes (zucchini), cut into 24 long strips lengthways (I used one yellow and one green)
salt
360 g (2¼ cups) seasoned sushi rice (cooked weight, see pages 22–23)
soy sauce, to serve

TOPPINGS
250 g (9 oz) mixed white and brown crab meat
3 red radishes, finely diced
1 tablespoon finely chopped dill
½ Braeburn apple, thinly sliced and soaked in lightly salted water to prevent it going brown

1. Place the courgette (zucchini) strips on a plate, sprinkle some salt over and leave for 10 minutes to draw the water out. Rinse off the salt and wipe off any excess water with paper towels.

2. Mix together the crab meat, radishes and dill in a small bowl.

3. Wet your hand in water to stop the rice sticking to it. Take a tablespoon (15 g/ ½ oz) of sushi rice and gently shape it into an oval ball. Repeat to make 24 balls. Set aside.

4. Wrap each rice ball with a courgette (zucchini) strip.

5. Top with apple slices and the crab meat mixture. Serve with the soy sauce.

GUNKAN MAKI

NORI-WRAPPED RICE TOPPED WITH TUNA TARTARE

When slicing fish to make maki sushi, you always end up with small leftover pieces, and this simple recipe is the perfect way to use them. Add some freshly chopped chives for flavouring and to balance out the colours, and you have some beautiful-looking, tasty sushi.

MAKES 24

360 g (2¼ cups) seasoned sushi rice (cooked weight, see pages 22-23)
4 sheets of nori
wasabi paste
soy sauce, to serve

TOPPINGS
360 g (13 oz) sashimi-quality tuna, finely chopped
5 g (¼ cup) finely chopped chives, plus extra to serve

1. To make tuna tartare, mix the tuna and chives together in a small bowl.

2. Cut each sheet of nori into six long strips, each 3.5 x 17 cm (1½ x 6¾ in). You will need 24 strips in total.

3. Wet your hand in water to stop the rice sticking to it. Take a tablespoon (15 g / ½ oz) of sushi rice and gently shape it into an oval ball. Repeat to make 24 balls. Set aside.

4. Wrap each rice ball with a nori strip. Close the end with a grain of rice to seal.

5. Place the wasabi paste on the rice and top with the tuna tartare. Sprinkle with extra chopped chives and serve them immediately with soy sauce for dipping. The nori will become soggy if left for too long.

KAZARI SUSHI
SHIKAI (FOUR SEAS)

When Great Britain hosted the Olympics in 2012, I was commissioned to make a portrait of Team Japan in A0 size (841 x 1189 mm / 33 x 47 in) moulded sushi. I was flown to Tokyo especially to learn how to master the art of kazari sushi, and what an incredible experience it was! Kazari sushi, which means 'decorative sushi', are traditionally made for celebrations but also for chefs to showcase their skills. This particular example represents four seas ('shikai') with the four bands of nori as four ocean waves coming from four different directions, circling an island in the middle.

MAKES 4 ROLLS

1 cooked beetroot (beet) in vinegar
240 g (1½ cups) seasoned sushi rice
   (cooked weight, see pages 22–23)
4 baby courgettes (zucchini) or
   cucumber, about 2 cm (¾ in) thick
4 sheets of nori, cut in half
1 carrot, cut into fine strips
   (see page 26)

1. To make pink rice, mix the beetroot (beet) with the rice to colour it evenly. Remove the beetroot (beet) when the rice has become sakura (cherry blossom) pink. (The beetroot is only used to colour the rice so after use, the beetroot can be enjoyed in a salad.)

2. Place the courgettes (zucchini) in a line at one short edge of a half-sheet of nori. Roll the nori over once to enclose the courgettes (zucchini). Spread the pink rice over the remainder of the nori sheet, leaving a blank space of about 1 cm (½ in) at the far end. Roll the courgette (zucchini) to the end of the nori so it looks like the courgette (zucchini) is surrounded by a layer of pink rice.

3. Seal the roll by pressing the blank edge of nori to the roll, leaving it lying on that edge for 3 minutes. It will stick due to the moist rice. In the meantime, make three more rolled courgettes (zucchini) in the same way.

4. Carefully cut one roll lengthways into quarters, slicing through the middle of the courgette (zucchini). Turn the pieces so that the rounded edges face inwards, forming a block. Stuff the gap in the centre with carrot strips.

5. Carefully roll the block in nori, so that all the cut edges are covered with nori, holding the rice in place. Seal the ends of the nori together by placing it sealed-side down for 3 minutes. In the meantime, make the remaining rolls in the same way.

6. To cut each roll, wipe the knife with a wet towel, then slice into four pieces. Serve cut-side up.

伝統的な寿司
TRADITIONAL MOULDED SUSHI

TEMARI
KOBUJIME (CURED SEA BASS)

Temari are little balls of sushi which are very quick to make. They look pretty as canapés, and here I top them with sea bass sashimi, which makes them look like cherry blossom. The sea bass is cured in kombu, the king of seaweed and a pillar of Japanese cuisine due to its high umami content. Curing sashimi in kombu draws out the water from the fish, giving it a better texture and helping to preserve it for longer. This curing technique is widely used in Japan for other white fish and vegetables.

FOR 24 BALLS

2 fillets of sashimi-quality sea bass, skinned and pin-boned

2 tablespoons sake

4 sheets kombu, 9 x 20 cm (3½ x 8 in) – flat kombu sheets are suitable

360 g (2¼ cups) seasoned sushi rice (cooked weight, see pages 22–23)

dill fronds

ponzu sauce (see page 38), to serve

1. To cure the sea bass, first sprinkle the sake on both sides of the kombu to reconstitute it. Thinly slice the sea bass diagonally, then place the pieces between two sheets of kombu. Wrap it tightly in clingfilm (plastic wrap) and refrigerate for 2 hours. This is the quick way to cure the fish. To cure the fish overnight, place the whole fillet between the kombu, then slice after curing, skin-side down, slicing diagonally from the head to tail.

2. To shape the temari, wet your hand in water to stop the rice sticking to it. Take a tablespoon (15 g/ ½ oz) of sushi rice and gently shape it into a small rice ball. Repeat to make 24 balls in total.

3. Place a 30-cm (12-in) square of clingfilm (plastic wrap) on a flat surface. Place a slice of sea bass in the centre, add a dill frond and put a sushi rice ball on top.

4. Gather the clingfilm (plastic wrap) up around the rice ball, then gently twist the film to seal the rice and fish together.

5. Unwrap the rice ball and place on a plate. Repeat with the remaining fish and rice balls.

6. Serve with the ponzu sauce.

OSHI SUSHI
MOSAIC SUSHI RICE PRESSED IN A LUNCHBOX

The most difficult part of this recipe is to find a box of the right dimensions! The making of the sushi itself is relatively easy, but it does require quite a bit of attention to detail. It's all about making a balanced but elaborate composition with simple yet delicious and fresh toppings. A Mondrianesque lunchbox, because you're worth it!

SERVES 2

600 g (4 cups) seasoned multi-grain sushi rice (cooked weight, see pages 22–24)
pickled ginger, to serve
wasabi, to serve
soy sauce, to serve

TOPPINGS
¼ cucumber
1 red radish
80 g (3 oz) smoked salmon
80 g (3 oz) sashimi-quality tuna
4 slices of egg roll (see pages 36–37)
4 steamed prawns (shrimp), butterfly-cut (see page 17)
2 teaspoons salmon roe
garnishes such as chives, dill, baby shiso leaves, edible flowers (optional)

TIP

All the toppings need to be cut into thin squares. I suggest you work out the dimensions of your box and cut the toppings to fit. The two boxes I used here measure 8 x 23 cm, and 5 cm high (3 x 9 in, and 2 in high) and 12 x 14 cm, and 5 cm high (4¾ x 5½ in, and 2 in high).

1. Cut the cucumber into sticks and thinly slice the red radish. Cut the smoked salmon, tuna and egg roll into even-sized squares (see tip, left).

2. Place the sushi rice into your lunchbox or bento box, press it down well and flatten the surface.

3. Place your chosen toppings on top of the rice in a mosaic pattern.

4. Garnish with the dill, chives or other herbs and serve with the pickled ginger, wasabi and soy sauce.

OSHI SUSHI

SUKO SUSHI

This recipe is very close to my heart as it came from my grandmother. She used to make this on special occasions – it's a tradition dating back 500 years when farmers from my region in Kyushu would prepare this as an offering to the local lords to show them their affection and gratitude. It was made with the renowned Shiroishi local rice and topped with freshly caught fish from the nearby Ariake Sea. A celebratory recipe indeed, and one that helped my grandmother to live until her 103rd birthday!

SERVES 4

800 g (5 cups) seasoned sushi rice (cooked weight, see pages 22–23)
9 cooked prawns (shrimp) (see vinegared prawns, page 94)
8 mangetout (snow peas), cut into thin strips and blanched
¼ carrot, cut with a maple leaf cutter and blanched

TUNA FLAKES (SOBORO)
60 g (2 oz) can of tuna in oil
1 tablespoon sake
½ tablespoon sugar
1 tablespoon dark soy sauce

EGG RIBBONS (KINSHI TAMAGO)
2 eggs
1 teaspoon sugar
a pinch of salt
a little vegetable oil, for frying

1. To make the tuna flakes, drain the can of tuna, reserving 1 tablespoon of the oil. Fry the tuna with the reserved oil, sake, sugar and soy sauce, stirring with four chopsticks to make fine flakes (or use a whisk). Reduce the heat to low, then stir constantly until the liquid has evaporated – this can take up to 8 minutes. Set aside to cool.

2. To make the thin egg ribbons (see page 36), mix the eggs, sugar and salt in a bowl. Heat a frying pan (skillet) over a medium heat and add a little oil soaked into a paper towel to grease the pan. Pour in a quarter of egg, tilting the pan to make an even sheet. When the underside has cooked, turn it over to cook the reverse side for a second, then slide onto a plate. Use a paper towel to blot away any excess oil. Repeat to make another three sheets. Cut the egg sheets in half, then roll up and slice finely into ribbons.

3. Spread the sushi rice in a container and press down evenly. The depth of the rice should be about 1.5 cm (⅝ in), and I used a container measuring 21 x 21 cm (8¼ x 8¼ in).

4. Using a knife, divide the sushi rice into squares of about 7 cm (2¾ in). Garnish with the tuna soboro, egg ribbons, prawns (shrimp), mangetout (snow peas) strips and maple-leaf shaped carrot.

OSHI SUSHI
PORK AND EGG SOBORO

This oshi sushi recipe is served in the traditional oshibako mould, which is used to press the sushi. Nowadays plastic oshibako are often used, but I think it's best to use wooden ones. This style of sushi first appeared in the middle of the Edo period (1603-1868), and was especially popular in Kansai region. This easy-to-take-home type of sushi is simple to make and you can experiment with all sorts of toppings of your choice. For this recipe, I use traditional soboro-style ingredients in three colours, with flavours that balance and complement one another. To make a successful soboro (scramble), use four cooking chopsticks for fine flakes or simply use a whisk for the same result!

SERVES 4

**800 g (5 cups) seasoned sushi rice
(cooked weight, see pages 22-23)**
**12 mangetout (snow peas),
blanched, finely sliced**

PORK SOBORO
250 g (9 oz) minced (ground) pork
2 tablespoons sake
2 tablespoons mirin
2½ tablespoons smooth red miso
2 teaspoons sugar
1 teaspoon freshly grated ginger

EGG SOBORO
2 large (US extra large) eggs
1 teaspoon sugar
a pinch of salt
vegetable oil

TIP
I used a box measuring 24 x 7 cm, and 5.5 cm high (9½ x 2¾ in, and 2¼ in high), see page 12. Alternatively, you could use a baking tin (pan) lined with clingfilm (plastic wrap).

1. To make the pork soboro, heat a medium saucepan, add the pork and stir over a medium heat using four chopsticks (or a whisk) to break any lumps. Add the sake, mirin, red miso and sugar, then continue stirring until all the liquid evaporates. Add the ginger and stir for another minute. Set aside.

2. To make the egg soboro, break the eggs into a mixing bowl, add the sugar and salt, then mix well. Heat a small saucepan over a medium heat and add a little oil soaked into a paper towel to grease the pan. Pour the egg mixture into the pan and stir using four chopsticks (or a whisk) to make fine scrambled egg. Set aside.

3. If using a wooden mould, soak it in water for about 10 minutes to avoid the rice sticking to the surface. Otherwise, line the mould with clingfilm (plastic wrap) to make it easier to handle the rice.

4. Pack the sushi rice into the bottom of mould. Flatten the surface of the rice. Add the toppings, creating a pattern of your choice on top of the rice.

5. Press the rice and toppings by placing the lid in the mould. Leave to set for 20 minutes.

6. Remove the mould and slice into a suitable size to serve.

OSHI SUSHI
BATTERA SUSHI (PICKLED MACKEREL)

This style of pressed sushi comes from the Kansai region and uses cooked or cured fish (never raw), which means you can keep it for up to 2 days. Pickled mackerel is the most loved and famous of oshi sushi, and is mostly eaten in autumn and winter when the fish is at its fattest. At other times the fish will be leaner, requiring less pickling time.

MAKES 2 ROLLS

200–300 g (1¼–2 cups) seasoned sushi rice (cooked weight, see pages 22–23)

1 tablespoon white sesame seeds

20 g (¾ oz) pickled ginger, finely chopped

4 shiso leaves, cut in half

4 red radishes, grated

PICKLED MACKEREL

2 fresh mackerel fillets

2 tablespoons fine sea salt

PICKLING SEASONING

100 ml (½ cup) rice vinegar

2 teaspoons sugar

1. To make the shime saba pickled mackerel, sprinkle both sides of the mackerel fillets with the sea salt. Set aside for 3–5 hours, for the salt to dissolve, the water to drain and the fishy smell to abate. (The time depends on the size of the fish. This recipe photo used relatively small mackerel and took about 3 hours.)

2. Rinse the salt from the fillets and wipe off any excess water.

3. Pickle the mackerel in the vinegar and sugar mixture for 2 hours. Remove the fillet from the pickling mixture, and pat dry with paper towel. To avoid over-pickled mackerel, remove the fillets from the pickling seasoning, wrap in clingfilm (plastic wrap) and store for up to 2 days in the fridge.

4. Pin-bone the fillet (using tweezers, see page 12), and peel the translucent, very thin skin from the head towards the tail.

5. Mix the seasoned sushi rice and white sesame seeds. Cover a bamboo mat with clingfilm (plastic wrap). Place the mackerel outer side down in the centre of the mat. Top with pickled ginger and shiso leaves. Wet your hand in water to stop the rice sticking to it. Shape a handful (100–150 g/¾–1 cup) of sushi rice along the fillet.

6. Roll the bamboo mat to stick the rice to the mackerel. Wrap in clingfilm (plastic wrap) for 20 minutes at room temperature to set. Unwrap, then cut the roll into bite-sized pieces, wiping the knife with a wet towel every time you cut. Top each piece with grated radish to serve.

CHAKIN SUSHI
SUSHI PARCEL

Chakin sushi are little sushi parcels traditionally made for Japanese Tea Ceremonies. These elegant sushi bites wrapped in their fine egg crepe and tied with a thin string of chive certainly have a celebratory look to them and will look stunning on a party menu or even in your bento box.

FOR 4 PARCELS

2 dried shiitake mushrooms
1 tablespoon dark soy sauce
1 tablespoon mirin
a pinch of sugar
a pinch of salt
5-cm (2-in) piece of cucumber, diced into small cubes
200 g (1¼ cups) seasoned sushi rice (cooked weight, see pages 22–23)
⅓ carrot, finely chopped and blanched

20 g (¾ oz) peeled and cooked prawns (shrimp), diced into small pieces
2 teaspoons yuzu zest (or citrus fruit such as lemon or orange if yuzu is not available)
4 whole chive stems

EGG SHEET
2 large (US extra large) eggs
1 teaspoon caster (superfine) sugar
a pinch of salt
vegetable oil, for frying

1. Soak the shiitake in 200 ml (1 cup) water for 30 minutes to reconstitute them, then remove from the water and squeeze out any excess water (keep the water as it will be used as stock). Discard the stems and then finely chop the shiitake mushrooms.

2. Place 100 ml (½ cup) shiitake stock, soy sauce, mirin and a pinch of sugar in a small saucepan, add the shiitake, then bring to the boil. Reduce the heat to low and simmer until the liquid has evaporated.

3. Sprinkle a pinch of salt on the cucumber and rub, leave for 10 minutes, then rinse and squeeze out the excess water.

4. To make a thin egg sheet, break the eggs into a mixing bowl, add the sugar and salt, then mix well. Heat a 24-cm (9½-in) non-stick frying pan (skillet) to medium heat, add a little oil soaked into a paper towel to wipe off the pan (see pages 36–37). Pour in a quarter of egg, tilting the pan to make an even sheet. When the surface has cooked, turn it over to cook the reverse side for a second, then slide onto a plate. Use the paper towel to remove the excess oil. Repeat to make three more sheets.

5. Mix the sushi rice, mushrooms, carrot, cucumber, prawns (shrimp) and zest in a bowl.

6. Dip the chives in boiling water for just a second, then rinse in cold water to stop the cooking process.

7. Shape the rice mixture into four round balls and place each ball in the centre of an egg sheet. Wrap and tie with a chive ribbon.

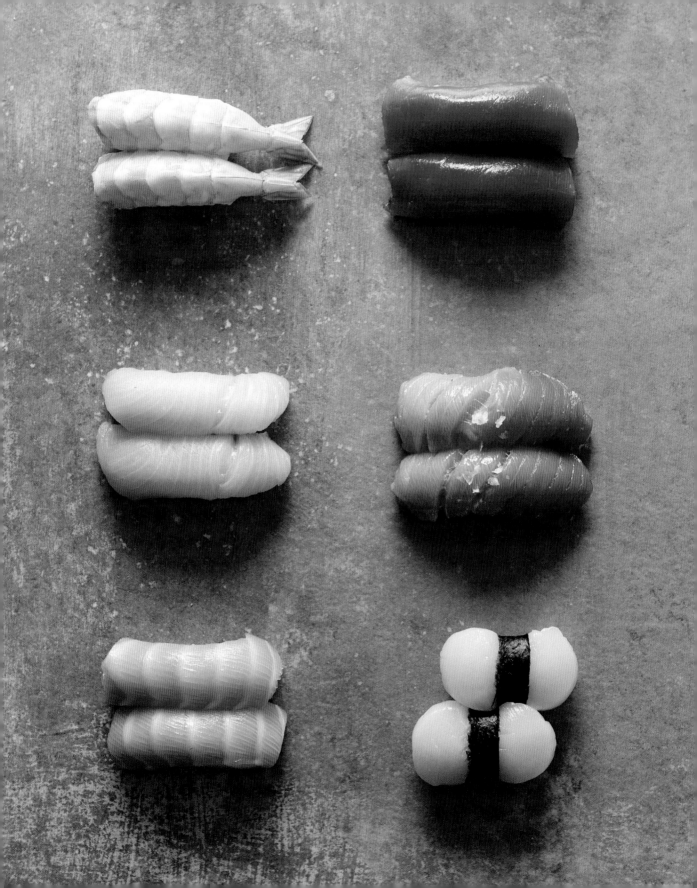

NIGIRI

This is the most refined style of sushi. You are probably familiar with it, but did you know it started being served on street stalls hundred years ago in the Edo Period (1603-1868), when it was the equivalent of today's fast food! As for the etiquette, it is okay to eat nigiri with your fingers, but make sure you only dip the fish in the soy sauce and not the rice!

PRAWN

MAKES 20

20 raw king prawns (jumbo shrimp), in their shells
100 ml (½ cup) sushi vinegar (see page 21)
150 ml (²/₃ cup) cold water
300 g (2 cups) seasoned sushi rice (cooked weight, see pages 22-23)
wasabi paste (optional)

1. Remove the heads from the prawns (shrimp) and insert a 15-cm (6-in) wooden skewer from the head along the belly to the tail.

2. Bring a large saucepan of water to the boil, add the prawns (shrimp) on their skewers, and cook for 2½ minutes until the flesh turns white and the shells turn pink. Remove from the pan and dip into cold water to stop the cooking process.

3. Once cooled, remove the skewers from the prawns (shrimp) by turning the skewer slowly. Remove the shell but keep the tail part on.

4. Score the centre of belly lengthways until the knife reaches at the back of prawn (shrimp), but not cutting all the way through. Open out the flesh, then devein (see page 17) and wash in cold water to clean.

5. Cut the edge of the tail to make it look like V shape.

6. Mix the sushi vinegar and water in a small bowl. Add the prawns (shrimp) and let them pickle for 20 minutes. Remove from the vinegar and drain. The prawns (shrimp) can then be kept for 2-3 days in the fridge.

7. To shape, wet your hand in water to stop the rice sticking to it. This makes it much easier to handle the rice. Take a tablespoon (15 g/½ oz) of sushi rice and gently shape it to a small oval ball. Make 20 balls.

8. Top the rice balls with the prawns (shrimp) (see page 34). Place a little wasabi paste between the rice and prawn (shrimp) if you like it hot!

HAMACHI (YELLOWTAIL)

MAKES 20

300 g (2 cups) seasoned sushi rice
   (cooked weight, see pages 22–23)
300 g (10½ oz) sashimi-quality
   hamachi, sliced thinly across
   the grain into 20 pieces
ponzu sauce (see page 38),
   to serve

AKAMI (TUNA)

MAKES 20

300 g (2 cups) seasoned sushi rice
   (cooked weight, see pages 22–23)
300 g (10½ oz) sashimi-quality
   akami (tuna), sliced thinly across
   the grain into 20 pieces
soy sauce, to serve

1. To shape, wet your hand in water to stop the rice sticking to it. This makes it much easier to handle the rice. Take a tablespoon (15 g / ½ oz) of sushi rice and gently shape it to a small oval ball. Make 20 balls.

2. Top the rice with the fish (see page 34). Place a little wasabi paste between the rice and fish if you like it hot!

TORO (FATTY TUNA)

MAKES 20

300 g (2 cups) seasoned sushi rice
   (cooked weight, see pages 22–23)
300 g (10½ oz) sashimi-quality
   toro (fatty tuna), sliced thinly
   across the grain into 20 pieces
sea salt, for sprinkling over the
   tuna just before serving

SALMON

MAKES 20

300 g (2 cups) seasoned sushi rice
   (cooked weight, see pages 22–23)
300 g (10½ oz) sashimi-quality
   salmon, sliced thinly across
   the grain into 20 pieces
soy sauce, to serve

SCALLOP

MAKES 20

300 g (2 cups) seasoned sushi rice
   (cooked weight, see pages 22–23)
20 sashimi-quality scallops
   (see page 17)
yuzu kosho (see page 38)
nori strips (see page 29)
soy sauce, to serve

1. To butterfly the scallops, place on a chopping board and score around the side of the scallop with the knife blade held parallel to the board. Slice almost all the way through the scallop, then open it out.

2. Wet your hand in water to stop the rice sticking to it. This makes it much easier to handle the rice. Take a tablespoon (15 g / ½ oz) of sushi rice and gently shape it to a small oval ball. Make 20 balls.

3. Top each rice ball with a scallop, placing a little yuzu kosho paste between the rice and scallop if you like it hot. Tie with a nori strip, closing it on the underside.

創作寿司
CREATIVE MOULDED SUSHI

SUSHI DOUGHNUTS

Sushi evolution is endless, and these sushi doughnuts are easy and fun to make. Colourful, playful and also very healthy, it's like biting into a rainbow! I also created the colourful rice base with matcha for green and beetroot (beet) for pink. These are great to serve at a party. You will need a 6-hole silicone doughnut mould.

MAKES 6

300 g (2 cups) seasoned sushi rice (cooked weight, see pages 22-23)
a pinch of matcha powder
a small piece of pickled beetroot (beet)
30 g (1 oz) sashimi-quality salmon, thinly sliced
30 g (1 oz) sashimi-quality sea bass, thinly sliced
30 g (1 oz) sashimi-quality tuna, thinly sliced
2 cucumber slices, sprinkled with a pinch of salt, then any excess water patted off
10 g (2 teaspoons) garden peas, blanched, cooled in cold water, drained
10 g (⅓ oz) yuzu-flavoured tobiko (flying fish roe), or other type of tobiko if yuzu is not available
10 g (⅓ oz) lumpfish caviar
6 lettuce or shiso leaves, to serve
soy sauce, to serve

1. Divide the rice evenly into three separate bowls. Leave one bowl of rice plain. Colour the second bowl green by stirring through a pinch of matcha powder. Colour the third bowl pink with the pickled beetroot (beet) - aim for a soft shade of pink like cherry blossom and remove the beetroot (beet) from the rice before the pink becomes too intense.

2. Place a mixture of the sashimi and cucumber side by side in the doughnut moulds. If you are using a non-silicone mould, wet the surface of moulds before adding the toppings or rice or simply line the moulds with clingfilm (plastic wrap) to prevent the sushi sticking.

3. Put the garden peas, tobiko and caviar in the gaps between the sashimi and cucumber.

4. Gently press the sushi rice into the moulds and flatten the top surface. Leave to rest for 10 minutes.

5. Place a large serving tray on top of the doughnut mould, then turn upside-down and remove the mould. The doughnuts will tip out onto the tray.

6. You could give your guests chopsticks for eating the doughnuts, but if you wish to serve them as finger food, then place each doughnut on top of a lettuce or shiso leaf (or alternatively place in a quartered sheet of nori) to make it easy to hold.

SUSHI BOMB
SPICY PORK AND KIMCHI

The most indulgent sushi, and to be eaten using both hands as you'll want to take the biggest bite possible! The kimchi, pork and runny egg yolk combination is not for the faint-hearted, but you won't mind getting messy as the taste is worth it!

MAKES 2 BOMBS

200 g (7 oz) pork shoulder, thinly sliced across the grain
2 large (US extra large) eggs
1 tablespoon vegetable oil
2½ sheets of nori
500 g (3 cups) seasoned sushi rice (cooked weight, see pages 22–23)
4 baby gem lettuce
80 g (1 cup) kimchi

SPICY BARBECUE SAUCE

2 tablespoons dark soy sauce
1 tablespoon mirin
1 tablespoon clear honey
1 teaspoon gochujang miso (Korean red chilli miso)
½ Braeburn apple, grated
1 teaspoon freshly grated ginger
2 garlic cloves, grated

1. Mix all the ingredients for the barbecue sauce in a bowl. Add the pork and marinade for 30 minutes.

2. Meanwhile, bring 1.5 litres (6 cups) water to the boil in a medium-sized saucepan. Carefully add the eggs into the water with a slotted spoon to prevent them from breaking. Boil for exactly 7 minutes (for runny egg yolks) over a medium-high heat.

3. Transfer the eggs to a bowl of cold water, then run under cold water to cool them quickly. When cooled, peel the eggs carefully. Set aside.

4. Heat a frying pan (skillet) over a medium heat. Add the vegetable oil, pork and the marinade and fry for about 5 minutes until all the sauce has evaporated.

5. Line a 15-cm (6-in) mixing bowl with clingfilm (plastic wrap). Place one sheet of nori carefully inside the bowl (try not to break the nori as it is dry).

6. Divide the rice into quarters and put a quarter at the bottom of the bowl. Press gently, then place some lettuce leaves on top, followed by half the pork, a peeled egg and half the kimchi. Cover with another quarter of the rice. Gently flatten the rice, then wrap the edges of the nori over the rice, adding a quarter-sheet to cover the gap.

7. Wrap the bomb in the clingfilm (plastic wrap) lining the bowl, then place upside-down to rest for 10 minutes. The nori will become moist from the rice and will stick together, sealing the bomb. Make a second bomb in the same way.

8. To serve, slice the bomb in half vertically to reveal the mouthwatering layers.

SUSHI BOMB
GRILLED SALMON AND SALMON ROE

With its beautifully seasoned salmon and umami-rich salmon roe, this is a more delicate and elegant version of the sushi bomb on the previous page. The miso-marinated fish with a little twist of orange fragrance wrapped in herby rice gives an explosion of flavour when you bite it. I had sashimi salmon leftover from another recipe, so I preserved it in miso so that it would last another day.

MAKES 2 BOMBS

200 g (7 oz) salmon fillet,
   diced or sliced
salt
2 shiso leaves, finely chopped
5 sprigs of dill, finely chopped
500 g (3 cups) seasoned sushi rice
   (cooked weight, see pages 22–23)
2 sheets of nori
10 g (⅓ oz) salmon roe

MARINADE
120 g (4 oz) saikyo miso
   (white sweet miso)
60 ml (4 tablespoons) mirin
1 tablespoon orange zest

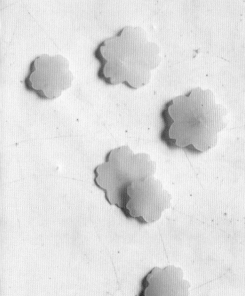

1. To marinate the salmon, sprinkle it with salt and leave for 20 minutes. Wipe off any excess water from the fish with paper towel.

2. To make the miso marinade, combine the saikyo miso and mirin in a bowl and add the orange zest.

3. Place half the marinade on a piece of clingfilm (plastic wrap), then lay the salmon in the middle, spread the remaining marinade on top of the salmon, then wrap the clingfilm (plastic wrap) around to seal. Leave for at least 2 hours or overnight in the fridge.

4. Preheat the oven to 170°C (350°F) Gas 4. Gently wipe the miso off the fish and place on a baking sheet. Bake in the preheated oven for about 10 minutes (depends on the thickness of salmon) until cooked. Gently break the fillet into pieces and set aside.

5. Line a 15-cm (6-in) mixing bowl with clingfilm (plastic wrap). Place one sheet of nori carefully inside the bowl (try not to break the nori as it is dry).

6. Mix the chopped shiso and dill leaves with the rice. Divide the rice into quarters and put a quarter at the bottom of the bowl. Press gently, then place a quarter of the salmon pieces on top, add the salmon roe at the centre of salmon, then add another quarter of the salmon to cover the roe. Cover with another quarter of the rice. Gently flatten the rice, then wrap the edges of the nori over the rice.

7. Wrap the bomb in the clingfilm (plastic wrap) lining the bowl, then place upside-down to rest for 10 minutes. The nori will become moist from the rice and will stick together, sealing the bomb. Make a second bomb in the same way.

8. To serve, slice the bomb in half vertically to reveal the layers.

SUSHI SANDWICHES
GANMODOKI (TOFU PATTY)

Ganmodoki were initially prepared in Zen Buddhist temples as a substitute for meat but their popularity soon spread. Usually Japanese temple cuisine (called 'shojin ryori') is vegan and does not allow the use of the onion family of vegetables. However, for this version, I add a spring onion (scallion) to give more flavour and crunchy pickled daikon for texture. These patties are packed with flavour and make a substantial filling in rice sandwiches.

MAKES 4

1 teaspoon dried hijiki seaweed
200 g (7 oz) firm tofu
½ large (US extra large) egg, beaten
10 g (¼ cup) panko breadcrumbs
½ tablespoon saikyo miso (white sweet miso)
½ teaspoon kombu kelp stock powder
1 spring onion (scallion), chopped
½ teaspoon freshly grated ginger
20 g (¾ oz) carrot, finely chopped
20 g (¾ oz) edamame beans or garden peas
vegetable oil, for deep frying
400 g (2½ cups) seasoned brown sushi rice (cooked weight, see pages 22–24)
20 g (¾ oz) pickled daikon, diced
kabayaki sauce (see page 38)
4 sheets of nori

1. Soak the hijiki in 500 ml (2 cups) of water for 10 minutes to reconstitute it. Drain well and set aside.

2. Drain the tofu, then wrap in paper towels to remove any excess water. Break the tofu into small pieces. Wrap again in paper towels and squeeze the tofu to remove as much water as possible.

3. Mash the tofu by hand in a large mixing bowl. Add the egg, panko, white miso, kombu kelp stock powder, spring onion (scallion) and grated ginger. Mix well. Once combined, add the hijiki, carrot and edamame. Mix gently until evenly combined.

4. Lightly wet your hands in water and form the mixture into four equal-sized patties about 2 cm (¾ in) thick. Set aside.

5. Heat the oil in a deep pan and deep fry the patties, two at a time, for 2–3 minutes or until golden brown. Don't put all in the oil at once; this will cause the temperature to drop and will make the vegetables mushy and not cook properly. Remove from the oil and drain on paper towels or a baking rack.

6. Line a square mould (8 x 8 cm, and 3.5 cm high/3¼ x 3¼ in, and 1½ in high) with clingfilm (plastic wrap) to prevent the sushi rice sticking (or use a square plastic container).

7. Divide the rice into eight and spread one portion in the base of the mould. Flatten the surface, place a patty in the centre and sprinkle with pickled daikon and a spoonful of kabayaki sauce. Cover with another portion of rice and flatten the surface.

8. Remove from the mould and turn the rice sandwich out onto the centre of a sheet of nori, then wrap it as if wrapping a gift (see page 35). Allow to rest for 10 minutes. Make another three in the same way.

SUSHI SANDWICHES
BLT / HAM AND CHEESE

Sushi sandwiches are as easy to make as normal sandwiches, but will appeal to those following a gluten-free diet as well as rice lovers. We all know that the marriage of ham and cheese works beautifully in a sandwich, as does BLT. This recipe will prove that replacing bread with rice is just as good! I've used multi-grain rice, which gives a lovely rosy tint to the rice but also adds texture, and brown rice for a healthier option - just like brown bread would do!

BLT

MAKES 4

500 g (3 cups) seasoned brown sushi rice (cooked weight, see pages 22-24)
4 slices of bacon, fried
1 tomato, cut into slices 1.5 cm (¾ in) thick
4 tablespoons mayonnaise
8 leaves of Little Gem lettuce
4 sheets of nori

1. Line a square mould (8 x 8 cm, and 3.5 cm high/3¼ x 3¼ in, and 1½ in high) with clingfilm (plastic wrap) to prevent the sushi rice sticking (you could also use a square plastic container).

2. Divide the rice into eight. Spread one portion at the bottom of the mould and flatten the surface.

3. Place the bacon and tomato on the rice, spread over the mayonnaise and top with lettuce.

4. Cover with another portion of sushi rice and flatten the surface.

5. Remove from the mould and turn the rice sandwich out onto the centre of a sheet of nori, then wrap it as if wrapping a gift (see page 35). Repeat to make another three sandwiches.

6. Wrap the rice sandwiches in clingfilm (plastic wrap), then rest for 10 minutes to let the nori settle. Cut in half to serve.

HAM AND CHEESE

MAKES 4

500 g (3 cups) seasoned multi-grain sushi rice (cooked weight, see pages 22-24)
4 slices of your choice of ham (such as honey roast ham or cured ham)
2 tablespoons wholegrain mustard
4 slices of your choice of cheese (such as Leerdammer, Emmenthal or Cheddar)
4 sheets of nori

1. Line a square mould (8 x 8 cm, and 3.5 cm high/3¼ x 3¼ in, and 1½ in high) with clingfilm (plastic wrap) to prevent the sushi rice sticking (you could also use a square plastic container).

2. Divide the rice into eight. Spread one portion at the bottom of the mould. Flatten the surface.

3. Place the ham on the rice, spread the mustard on top, then put the cheese on it.

4. Cover with another portion of sushi rice and flatten the surface.

5. Remove from the mould and turn the rice sandwich out onto the centre of a sheet of nori, then wrap it as if wrapping a gift (see page 35). Repeat to make another three sandwiches.

6. Wrap the rice sandwiches in clingfilm (plastic wrap), then rest for 10 minutes to let the nori settle. Cut in half to serve.

SUSHI SANDWICHES
CHICKEN KARAAGE

Chicken karaage is Japan's most loved fried chicken. Marinated in soy and mirin with garlic and ginger, it is great as a snack just after it has been made, but it also works well in rice sandwiches. For this recipe, I use sushi rice without sushi vinegar so you can enjoy the hot rice and crispy chicken combination.

MAKES 4

500 g (3 cups) hot sushi rice (cooked weight, see pages 22–23 but leave out the sushi vinegar)
40 g (¾ cup) thinly sliced red cabbage
4 sheets of nori

MARINADE
1 teaspoon freshly grated ginger
1 teaspoon freshly grated garlic
2 tablespoons dark soy sauce
1 tablespoon mirin
1 tablespoon sake

CHICKEN KARAAGE
2 boneless chicken thighs, skin on
4 tablespoons katakuriko (potato starch)
4 tablespoons plain (all-purpose) flour
rapeseed oil, for deep frying

1. Mix all the marinade ingredients together in a bowl. Cut each chicken thigh into 4–6 pieces, add to the bowl and marinate for at least 30 minutes (or up to 2 hours, if you have time).

2. Remove the chicken pieces from the bowl and drain any excess marinade. Mix together the katakuriko and flour, then use to coat the chicken pieces.

3. Heat the oil in a deep pan over a medium-high heat to 170°C/350°F. Deep fry the chicken for about 5 minutes until cooked through and crispy. Drain well.

4. Line a square mould (8 x 8 cm, and 3.5 cm high/3¼ x 3¼ in, and 1½ in high) with clingfilm (plastic wrap) to prevent the rice sticking (you could also use a square plastic container).

5. Divide the rice into eight. Spread one portion at the bottom of the mould. Flatten the surface. Place a quarter of the chicken on the rice and add a quarter of the red cabbage. Cover with another portion of the rice and flatten the surface.

6. Remove from the mould and turn the rice sandwich out onto the centre of a sheet of nori, then wrap it (see page 35). Repeat to make another three sandwiches.

7. Wrap the rice sandwiches in clingfilm (plastic wrap), then leave to rest for 10 minutes to let the nori settle.

8. Cut the sandwiches in half to serve.

SUSHI BURGER
CHICKEN TERIYAKI

The inspiration behind this recipe is Japan's popular fast-food restaurant MOS Burger and its famous rice burger, which features a bun made of rice. This is a great recipe for leftover rice. The only thing I add to it is a bit of katakuriko (or alternatively use cornflour/cornstarch) to make it all stick together. I then press it inside a ring to make buns which are pan-fried. As simple as that! Be sure to fry them until golden brown for a nice crunchy texture when you bite into your burger!

MAKES 4

4 boneless chicken thighs, skin on
2 tablespoons katakuriko
(potato starch)
1 tablespoon vegetable oil
a handful of wild rocket (arugula)
or salad leaves
1 medium tomato, sliced
120 g (½ cup) mayonnaise

RICE BUNS
600 g (4 cups) seasoned sushi rice
(cooked weight, see pages 22–23)
2 tablespoons katakuriko
(potato starch)
2 tablespoons vegetable oil

TERIYAKI SAUCE
3 tablespoons dark soy sauce
3 tablespoons sake
3 tablespoons mirin
1 tablespoon brown sugar

1. To make the rice buns, evenly mix the rice with the katakuriko, then divide the rice into eight portions.

2. Line a 9-cm (3½-in) ring mould with clingfilm (plastic wrap). Place one portion of rice on the film, then press down firmly.

3. Remove from the ring mould and set aside with another piece of clingfilm (plastic wrap) under the bun to stop it sticking to the surface. Repeat to make the remaining buns.

4. Heat the oil in a non-stick frying pan (skillet). Fry the buns for 3–4 minutes to brown and crisp each side. Transfer to a baking tray and cover with foil to keep them warm and to stop them drying out.

5. Mix the teriyaki sauce ingredients together, stirring until the sugar has dissolved. Set aside.

6. Lightly coat the chicken with the katakuriko. Heat a frying pan (skillet) over a medium heat and add the oil to the pan. Fry the chicken pieces, skin-side down, for 2–3 minutes until brown. Remove the chicken fat by tilting the pan to the side and soaking it up with a paper towel.

7. Turn the chicken over and add the teriyaki sauce to the pan. Stir to season and coat the chicken evenly. Simmer for 5–6 minutes on medium-high heat until the sauce thickens and the chicken is cooked through. Remove the chicken from the pan and slice into strips.

8. Layer four buns with rocket (arugula) leaves, tomato, mayonnaise and chicken teriyaki. Top each with another bun.

SUSHI BURGER
PANKO-BREADED HADDOCK

Fish partnered with a dollop of freshly made tartare sauce makes a wonderful filling to this sushi burger. In the Japanese version, I use panko breadcrumbs. The main difference to other breadcrumbs is that panko is made from bread without crusts, so its airy, large flakes give fried food a light, crunchy coating.

SERVES 4

4 haddock fillets
50 g (3½ tablespoons) plain (all-purpose) flour
1 large (US extra large) egg
100 g (2⅓ cups) panko breadcrumbs
vegetable oil, for frying
a handful of wild rocket (arugula)

RICE BUNS
600 g (4 cups) seasoned sushi rice (cooked weight, see pages 22-23)
2 tablespoons katakuriko (potato starch)
2 tablespoons vegetable oil
2 tablespoons soy sauce
2 tablespoons black sesame seeds

TARTARE SAUCE
2 large (US extra large) eggs, hard-boiled for 10 minutes
2 tablespoons finely chopped shallot
2 tablespoons finely chopped gherkins (pickles)
2 tablespoons freshly chopped parsley
4 tablespoons mayonnaise
2 teaspoons freshly squeezed lemon juice, plus wedges for serving
salt

1. To make the rice buns, evenly mix the rice with the katakuriko, then divide the rice into eight portions.

2. Line a 9-cm (3½-in) ring mould with clingfilm (plastic wrap). Place one portion of rice on the film, then press down firmly.

3. Remove from the ring mould and set aside with another piece of clingfilm (plastic wrap) under the bun to stop it sticking to the surface. Repeat to make the remaining buns.

4. Heat the oil in a non-stick frying pan (skillet). Fry the buns for 3-4 minutes until brown and crisp on each side. Brush one side of each bun with soy sauce for an aromatic flavour and fry for one minute. Transfer to a baking tray, sprinkle with the black sesame seeds and cover with foil to keep them warm and to stop them drying out.

5. To make the tartare sauce, finely chop the boiled eggs, then mix with the shallot, gherkins (pickles) and parsley in a small bowl. Add the mayonnaise and lemon juice and season with salt.

6. Dust the fish with the flour, and then dip into the beaten egg. Next, coat the fish with the panko. Sprinkle extra panko on top of each fillet to ensure they are fully coated. Refrigerate for 15 minutes to set.

7. To fry the fish, heat the oil in a heavy-based saucepan over a high heat to 170°C/350°F. To check that the oil is ready, drop a few panko breadcrumbs into the oil - if they float to the surface and sizzle, the oil is ready. Once the correct temperature has been reached, reduce the heat to medium. Deep fry the fish for 3 minutes on each side (depending on the thickness of fish), turning over a few times until golden brown. Drain the fish on paper towels or a baking rack.

8. Layer four buns with rocket (arugula) leaves, the fish and a spoonful of tartare sauce. Top each with another bun.

SUSHI BURGER
KINPIRA

Kinpira is the term for the method of stir-frying root vegetables in soy sauce and mirin. And by extension, it also refers to the traditional spicy, salty, sweet side dish often enjoyed with rice. Kinpira is addictive, and you'll find yourself eating most of it before assembling your burger! If you can't find renkon (lotus root), you can easily use parsnip.

SERVES 4

RICE BUNS
600 g (4 cups) seasoned brown sushi rice (cooked weight, see pages 22–24)
2 tablespoons katakuriko (potato starch)
2 tablespoons vegetable oil
8 x 5-cm (2-in) squares of nori

KINPIRA
300 g (10½ oz) renkon (lotus root)
1 carrot

SEASONINGS
1 tablespoon sesame oil
2 teaspoons brown sugar
2 tablespoons mirin
2½ tablespoons dark soy sauce

TO SERVE
1 teaspoon toasted white sesame seeds
shichimi spice (optional)

1. To make the rice buns, evenly mix the rice with the katakuriko, then divide the rice into eight portions.

2. Line a 9-cm (3½-in) ring mould with clingfilm (plastic wrap). Place one portion of rice on the film, then press down firmly.

3. Remove from the ring mould and set aside with another piece of clingfilm (plastic wrap) under the bun to stop it sticking to the surface. Repeat to make the remaining buns.

4. Heat the oil in a non-stick frying pan (skillet). Fry the buns for 3–4 minutes until brown and crisp on each side. Transfer to a baking tray and cover with foil to keep them warm and to stop them drying out.

5. Slice the renkon and carrot into thin round slices. Soak the renkon in vinegared water for about 10 minutes. This helps to remove any bitter flavour and stop it turning brown.

6. Heat a frying pan (skillet) and add the sesame oil. Fry the renkon and carrot. When all the vegetables are coated with oil, add the sugar, mirin and 2 tablespoons of dark soy sauce. Add 90 ml (⅓ cup) of water, bring to the boil and cover with a lid. Reduce the heat to medium and simmer for 4 minutes.

7. Take the lid off, add the rest of the dark soy sauce, then increase the heat and boil until the liquid has evaporated.

8. Stuff the buns with the kinpira renkon and a square of nori, top with sesame seeds and sprinkle over the shichimi if you like it hot.

SUSHI BURGER
KAKIAGE VEGETABLE AND PRAWN TEMPURA

Kakiage is a very popular form of tempura in Japan and is often enjoyed at home using whatever vegetables you have to hand. It works wonderfully well in a rice bun as it adds crunch, and here the multi-grain rice adds a delicious nutty flavour.

SERVES 4

RICE BUNS
600 g (4 cups) seasoned multi-grain sushi rice (cooked weight, see pages 22–24)
2 tablespoons katakuriko (potato starch)
2 tablespoons vegetable oil

KAKIAGE TEMPURA
1 onion, sliced into 1 cm (½ in) rings
1 carrot, peeled and thinly sliced into ribbons
8 raw king prawns (jumbo shrimp)
20 g (¾ oz) edamame beans, shelled

TEMPURA BATTER
1 large (US extra large) egg yolk
75 ml (5 tablespoons) iced water
2 tablespoons plain (all-purpose) flour, plus extra for dusting
1½ tablespoons katakuriko (potato starch)
vegetable oil, for frying

ANKAKE SAUCE
100 ml (½ cup) katsuobushi dashi stock
2 tablespoons mirin
2 tablespoons light soy sauce
½ tablespoon katakuriko (potato starch), mixed with 1 tablespoon cold water

TO SERVE
a handful of mixed salad leaves
shichimi spice (optional)

1. Make the rice buns as in steps 1–4 on page 114.

2. To make the ankake sauce, place the dashi stock, mirin and light soy sauce in a small saucepan and bring to the boil. Reduce the heat to low, stir the katakuriko mixture well if it has separated and pour slowly into the pan to thicken the sauce. Bring to the boil again, then remove from the heat.

3. To make the batter, mix the egg yolk and iced water in a medium bowl. Combine the flour and katakuriko, then add to the egg yolk mixture. Slowly mix the batter with chopsticks or a spoon. Don't worry if it looks lumpy – the key to crisp tempura is not to overmix the batter.

4. Place the vegetables and prawns (shrimp) in a large mixing bowl and lightly coat with a little extra flour. This will help the batter to stick better.

5. Pour vegetable oil to a depth of 3 cm (1¼ in) into a heavy saucepan and heat to 170–180°C (350–370°F). Drop in a small amount of the batter. If it sizzles and floats to the surface within a few seconds, the oil is ready and at the correct temperature. Reduce the heat to medium.

6. Coat the floured vegetables and prawns (shrimp) in the batter. Using a slotted spoon, take a spoonful of the ingredients, hold the spoon over the bowl for a moment to allow any extra batter to fall off, then gently drop the ingredients into the oil.

7. Deep fry the vegetables and prawns (shrimps) in batches for 2–3 minutes, or until golden brown. Don't put them all in the oil at once; this will cause the temperature to drop and will make the vegetables mushy and not cook properly. Remove from the oil and drain on paper towels or a baking rack.

8. Stuff the buns with salad leaves and kakiage tempura. Pour the ankake sauce over the top before adding the top bun. Sprinkle with shichimi if you like it hot.

MINI SUSHI CAKES
SUSHI RICE DECORATED WITH A VARIETY OF TOPPINGS

These lovely cakes look stunning for a canapé party, adding colour and creativity to your menu. They are extremely easy to make and take very little time once you have cooked the rice. I use beetroot (beet) and matcha as natural colourants to tint the rice, but you'll hardly notice the difference in taste, especially with the addition of the other ingredients.

MAKES 6

600 g (4 cups) seasoned sushi rice (cooked weight, see pages 22–23)
¼ teaspoon matcha powder
1 pickled beetroot (beet)
40 g (½ cup) garden peas, blanched, cooled in cold water, drained
120 g (4 oz) cooked and peeled prawns (shrimp)
60 g (2 oz) smoked salmon, sliced
6 slices of cucumber
a pinch of salt
kinshi tamago (egg ribbons, see page 36)
soy sauce, to serve

1. Divide the rice evenly into three separate bowls. Leave one bowl of rice plain. Colour the second bowl green by stirring through a pinch of matcha powder. Colour the third bowl pink with the pickled beetroot (beet) – aim for a soft shade of pink like cherry blossom and remove the beetroot from the rice before the pink becomes too intense.

2. Line and cover a 7-cm (2¾-in) ring mould with clingfilm (plastic wrap) to prevent the sushi rice sticking to the surface.

3. Divide each bowl of coloured rice into six portions.

4. Take one portion of rice (of whichever colour you like) and spread at the bottom of the mould, then flatten the surface. Scatter the peas and prawns (shrimp) on top, then cover with a different coloured portion of sushi rice and flatten the surface. Repeat to make another five cakes. Rest for 10 minutes.

5. To make the toppings, roll up the thin layers of salmon (if the slices are wide, cut into narrower lengths to allow them to sit on top of the sushi cakes). Loosen the top part of the roll so that it opens up like a flower.

6. Sprinkle a pinch of salt on the cucumber slices to make them wilt a little, then pat off any excess water and roll them up.

7. Place a large serving tray on top of the filled moulds, then turn upside-down. Remove the moulds and the clingfilm (plastic wrap).

8. To garnish the sushi cakes, place the egg strings on top and add the rolled smoked salmon and cucumber.

CHRISTMAS SUSHI

These will make you very popular when you host a Christmas party! Although they couldn't be simpler to make, they always attract so much attention. And if you don't have the right cookie cutters already, you'll easily find them in stores during the Christmas season. I used a 13-cm (5-in) tree cutter, a 9-cm (3½-in) holly leaf and a 7-cm (2¾-in) star.

MAKES 2 HOLLY LEAVES, 2 CHRISTMAS TREES AND 2 STARS

400 g (2½ cups) seasoned sushi rice (cooked weight, see pages 22–23)
1 pickled beetroot (beet)
2 teaspoons green nori flakes
20 mangetout (snow peas), blanched
mayonnaise
3 stems of redcurrants
1 okra, blanched, sliced
3 tablespoons tuna soboro (see page 84)
3 tablespoons egg soboro (see page 87)
soy sauce, to serve

1. For the pink rice, place a quarter of the sushi rice in a bowl and roll the beetroot (beet) on the rice to put the pink colour on the rice until it turns a pale pink, like a cherry blossom. Remove the beetroot (beet) from the rice before the colour becomes too intense.

2. Mix the remaining rice in a separate bowl with the green nori flakes.

3. Wet the cutters in a bowl of water to prevent the sushi rice sticking to the surface.

4. Take the nori-seasoned rice and spread inside the holly leaf and Christmas tree cutters. Add the pink rice to the star cutter. My cutters are 2.5 cm (1 in) tall and I filled them to the top. Press the rice to flatten the surface, then carefully remove the cutters.

5. To decorate the Christmas tree, place the mangetout (snow peas) horizontally on a chopping board. Cut them into lengths to fit across the width of the tree, cutting the ends at an angle if necessary. Spread the mayonnaise lightly on the rice, then carefully place the mangetout (snow peas) on top to match the shape. Garnish with redcurrants (as baubles) and okra (as the star at the top), sticking them in place with a dab of mayonnaise. Sprinkle the tuna soboro on the trunk of tree.

6. For the star, garnish with egg soboro.

7. For the holly leaf, add a few redcurrants to look like berries.

CELEBRATION SUSHI CAKE
SUSHI RICE DECORATED WITH A VARIETY OF TOPPINGS

This is a real celebration piece for special occasions. It is very easy to assemble, just like the mini sushi cakes on page 118. The trickiest part is to try and keep each layer even and flat, so they end up parallel when you take the mould off. Cut and serve as a regular cake, and enjoy the colours of the layers and the different tastes and textures. You can have fun decorating it with your own ideas - I made these roses from thin slices of pickled turnip!

SERVES 6-8

- **120 g (4 oz) sashimi-quality salmon, thinly sliced**
- **120 g (4 oz) sashimi-quality sea bass, thinly sliced**
- **800 g (5 cups) seasoned sushi rice (cooked weight, see pages 22-23), divided into two**
- **4 eggs, soboro (see page 87)**
- **120 g (4 oz) smoked salmon**
- **400 g (2½ cups) seasoned multi-grain sushi rice (cooked weight, see pages 22-24)**
- **3 tablespoons taramasalata**
- **½ avocado, sliced, with 1 teaspoon fresh lemon juice squeezed over**
- **120 g (4 oz) cooked and peeled prawns (shrimp)**
- **40 g (¼ cup) garden peas, blanched, cooled in cold water, drained**
- **40 g (1½ oz) salmon roe**
- **2 baby turnips, pickled (see page 151)**
- **2 sugarsnap peas, blanched, cooled in cold water, drained**
- **soy sauce, to serve**

1. Line and cover a 20-cm (8-in) cake tin (pan) with clingfilm (plastic wrap) to prevent the sushi rice sticking to it.

2. This will turn upside down at the end so start with the top layer. Place sashimi-quality salmon and sea bass over the base of the cake tin (pan) in a pretty arrangement.

3. Gently spread half of the seasoned plain sushi rice on top of the fish and flatten the surface.

4. Sprinkle half of the egg soboro (scrambled egg) over the rice in the cake tin (pan). Lay the smoked salmon on top.

5. Add the seasoned multi-grain sushi rice, gently press it down and flatten the surface.

6. Spread over the taramasalata, and scatter the avocado and prawns (shrimp) on top.

7. Mix the remaining plain sushi rice with garden peas and spread evenly on top of the prawns (shrimp).

8. Rest for 20 minutes in the refrigerator.

9. Put a large serving tray on top of the cake tin (pan) and turn it upside down. Carefully remove the tin (pan) and the clingfilm (plastic wrap).

10. To garnish the sushi cake, use a ring mould to place the remaining egg soboro in the centre, then garnish with spoons of salmon roe around the egg. To make the rose, roll up thin layers of pickled turnip, then gently loosen the top part of the roll with your fingers so that it opens up like a rose. Place the turnip roses and sugarsnap peas on top to complete the cake.

CRISPY SUSHI RICE
WITH SPICY TUNA AND AVOCADO

The inspiration behind this recipe is my friend Noriko who works as a sushi chef in a famous restaurant in London. The recipe was created to avoid wasting leftover sushi rice but it became so popular that her restaurant has to prepare more rice for this dish a day before! This recipe is magical – crispy outside and chewy and moist inside, and the best way to revive your second-day sushi rice and enjoy another delicious snack!

MAKES 32 PIECES

400 g (2½ cups) seasoned sushi rice (cooked weight, see pages 22–23)
50 g (6 tablespoons) plain (all-purpose) flour
vegetable oil, for deep frying

PICKLED CHERRY TOMATOES
32 cherry tomatoes
160 ml (¾ cup) rice vinegar
160 ml (¾ cup) mirin

TUNA TARTARE
200 g (7 oz) sashimi-quality tuna, finely diced
1 spring onion (scallion), finely sliced, soaked in water to remove bitterness, drained well
50 g (¼ cup) spicy mayo (see page 41)

AVOCADO TARTARE
1 avocado
2 teaspoons freshly squeezed lime juice
salt and freshly ground black pepper

1. Make a shallow cut in the skin of each tomato using the tip of a sharp knife (just to break the skin). Bring a pan of water to the boil. Place all the tomatoes in a sieve (strainer) and lower into the boiling water for 5 seconds. When the skin begins to peel, quickly remove the tomatoes from the pan and soak in iced water to stop the cooking process. Once cooled, remove the skins. Combine the rice vinegar and mirin in a bowl, add the skinned tomatoes and leave to marinate for at least 20 minutes or overnight.

2. For the crispy rice, cover a bamboo mat with clingfilm (plastic wrap) to stop the rice sticking to the surface. Wet your hand in water to stop the rice sticking to it. Take an apple-sized amount of rice and place on the mat. Shape the rice into a stick about 20 cm (8 in) long and 2.5 cm (1 in) thick. Roll the rice with the bamboo mat and press it very firmly. To make a square shape, press the side of the rolled rice and push the top at the same time to make sharp edges. Wrap the rice in clingfilm (plastic wrap) and rest in the fridge overnight – this makes the rice harder outside. Make more rolls with the remaining rice.

3. For the tuna tartare, combine all the ingredients just before serving. For the avocado tartare, mash the avocado, drizzle over the lime juice to prevent it discolouring and season with salt and pepper.

4. Cut each rice roll into eight cubes. Wipe off the knife with a wet towel between cuts as this helps to cut the roll cleanly. Heat the vegetable oil to a depth of 3 cm (1¼ in) in a heavy saucepan to 180°C/350°F over a high heat. Once the correct temperature has been reached, reduce the heat to medium.

5. Dust the rice cubes in flour, then deep fry for 2 minutes or until golden. Don't put them all in the oil at once because they will stick together. Remove from the oil and drain on paper towels.

6. Serve the rice while it is hot and crispy and dip in the tuna or avocado tartare. For canapés, skewer the tomatoes to the crispy rice cubes.

ちらし寿司と丼ぶり
DECONSTRUCTED SUSHI

DONBURI
KAISEN (FRESH SASHIMI ON A BOWL OF RICE)

If you are in the mood for sushi but do not want to concern yourself with precise fish slicing or maki rolling, then donburi (also known, more simply, as a bowl of rice with toppings) is the perfect solution. Seasoned sushi rice is served in a large bowl and topped with a variety of fresh fish and vegetables, so the sushi flavours are all there but without the lengthier preparation that comes with other types of sushi.

SERVES 4

800 g (5 cups) seasoned sushi rice (cooked weight, see pages 22–23)

TOPPINGS
240 g (8½ oz) sashimi-quality salmon
160 g (5½ oz) sashimi-quality tuna
100 g (3½ oz) sashimi-quality sea bass
100 g (3½ oz) cooked prawns (shrimp)
4 red radishes, shredded
4 shiso leaves
40 g (1½ oz) salmon roe

TO SERVE
pickled ginger
wasabi paste
soy sauce

1. Slice the salmon fillet into 16 slices, and the tuna and sea bass each into 12 slices. Be sure to slice across the grain to ensure that the fish is tender.

2. To serve, divide the sushi rice between four individual bowls and flatten the surface of the rice. Top with the salmon, tuna, sea bass and prawns (shrimp), arranged in overlapping slices.

3. Garnish with the shredded red radishes, shiso leaves and salmon roe.

4. Serve with pickled ginger as a palate cleanser, and wasabi and soy sauce to taste.

DONBURI
OYAKODO
(SALMON AND SALMON ROE)

Oyakodo literally means a 'parent and child' bowl of rice! One of the most loved donburi, this is traditionally served with a chicken and egg topping, but this fresh pescatarian version is just as delicious and moreish with the marinated salmon roe packed with umami flavours. Serve on a slightly warm bed of sushi rice to enjoy the flavours at their best, as the salmon fat will melt a little and the marinated sauce will be soaked up by the rice. If you love salmon, you'll find this simple and delicious feast addictive.

SERVES 4

400 g (2½ cups) seasoned sushi rice (cooked weight, see pages 22–23)

TOPPINGS
400 g (14 oz) sashimi-quality salmon
200 g (7 oz) marinated salmon roe (see page 70)
4 baby shiso leaves
slices of lime or lemon

TO SERVE
pickled ginger
wasabi paste
soy sauce
strips of nori (optional)

1. Slice the salmon into thin slices. Be sure to slice across the grain to ensure that the fish is tender.

2. Place the sushi rice in four individual bowls and flatten the surface of the rice. Top with sashimi salmon and salmon roe. Garnish with the baby shiso leaves and lime or lemon slices.

3. Serve with pickled ginger as a palate cleanser, and wasabi and soy sauce to taste. If you wish, sprinkle with nori strips for more flavour.

CLASSIC CHIRASHI SUSHI
SUSHI RICE DECORATED WITH A VARIETY OF TOPPINGS

Chirashi sushi, or 'scattered sushi', is a celebratory dish which is usually eaten for Hina-matsuri or Girls' Day on 3rd March or other occasions. It is technically easy but a little time-consuming to make, especially with this gomoku-style version which uses a variety of cooked ingredients. Every family has different style of chirashi and this is the classic one my mum used to make. It includes renkon (lotus root) which is known as a nutrient-rich food, high in vitamin C and minerals. It also gives a crunchy texture and unique decoration to the dish. Fresh lotus root is usually available in Asian grocery stores. If you wish, you could prepare the seasoned ingredients in advance and assemble them on the day of the celebration. I do assure you it is worth every bit of the effort!

SERVES 4

**800 g (5 cups) seasoned sushi rice
(cooked weight, see pages 22–23)**
**60 g (½ cup) carrot, finely chopped,
blanched**
kinshi tamago (see page 36)
**8 mangetout (snow peas), blanched,
cut into half diagonally**

First prepare the shiitake mushrooms, renkon and prawns (shrimp) as per the three recipes.

To assemble (see the photo overleaf), mix together the sushi rice, shiitake and chopped carrot in a 30-cm (12-in) sushi mixing bowl. Sprinkle the egg ribbons on top, then garnish with the renkon slices, prawns (shrimp) and mangetout (snow peas).

SHIITAKE MUSHROOMS

4 dried shiitake mushrooms
1½ tablespoons dark soy sauce
1½ tablespoons mirin
1 teaspoon sugar

1. Soak the shiitake mushrooms in 250 ml (1 cup) of water for 30 minutes to reconstitute them.

2. Remove the shiitake mushrooms from the water and squeeze out any excess water (keep the water as it will be used in the next step). Finely chop the shiitake mushrooms, discarding the stems.

3. Add 200 ml (¾ cup) shiitake stock, soy sauce, mirin and sugar to a small saucepan. Add the chopped shiitake, then bring to the boil. Reduce the heat to low and simmer until the liquid has evaporated. The mushrooms can then be stored in the fridge for a week.

RENKON

100 g (3½ oz) fresh renkon
   (lotus root)
1 tablespoon rice vinegar, mixed
   with 250 ml (1 cup) water
2 tablespoons sushi vinegar
   (see page 21), or a mixture
   of 1 tablespoon vinegar,
   1½ teaspoons sugar and
   a pinch of salt

1. Peel and slice the renkon into thin rounds. (Alternatively, to cut into flowers, cut a 3-4 cm/ 1¼-1½ in length of renkon, peel, then to make petals cut out a small strip from the outer edge between the holes, then slice.) Soak the slices in the rice vinegar and water mixture to stop them going brown.

2. Place the sushi vinegar in a small saucepan with 3½ tablespoons water. Bring to the boil, add the renkon slices and simmer for 2 minutes to keep the crunchiness. Remove the pan from the heat and leave the renkon to cool in the seasonings. The renkon can then be stored in the fridge for a week.

PRAWNS

8 raw king prawns (jumbo shrimp),
   shells on, heads removed
40 ml (2½ tablespoons) sushi
   vinegar (see page 21)

1. To devein the prawns (shrimp), insert a skewer at the tail near the back of the prawn (shrimp). Carefully pull out the vein. This will remove the black intestine without cutting the back of prawn (shrimp).

2. Bring a large saucepan of water to the boil, add the prawns (shrimp) and cook for 2-3 minutes until the flesh turns white and the shells turn bright orange. Remove from the pan, then dip the prawns (shrimp) into cold water to stop the cooking process.

3. Once cooled, drain the water and remove the shells, but keep the tail part on.

4. Trim the edge of the tail to make it look like V shape.

5. Mix the sushi vinegar with 6 tablespoons of cold water, add the prawns (shrimp) and leave to pickle for 20 minutes. Remove from the vinegar. The prawns (shrimp) can then be stored in the fridge for 2-3 days.

CHIRASHI
SMOKED MACKEREL

This is not a traditional chirashi that you would find in Japan, but purists would certainly not disapprove of it after tasting the delicious British smoked mackerel! This quick and easy meal recipe is something I created when I first moved to London. For a good balance of texture, I've added cucumber and toasted sesame seeds. Simple ingredients, but satisfying from the first mouthful.

SERVES 4

½ cucumber
¼ teaspoon fine salt
200 g (7 oz) smoked mackerel
    fillets, boneless, skinless
40 g (1½ oz) pickled ginger, finely
    chopped
1 spring onion (scallion), finely
    sliced
2 teaspoons finely chopped dill
2 tablespoons toasted white
    sesame seeds
800 g (5 cups) seasoned sushi rice
    (cooked weight, see pages 22–23)
1 sheet of nori, torn into pieces
dark soy sauce, to serve

1. Slice the cucumber as thinly as possible and sprinkle with salt. Rub the cucumber lightly and leave for 10 minutes. This will help to remove any excess water from the cucumber to keep it crisp.

2. Squeeze out any excess water from the cucumber by hand.

3. Break the smoked mackerel into small pieces.

4. Add the cucumber, smoked mackerel, pickled ginger, spring onion (scallion), dill and white sesame seeds to the rice. Combine well to spread the ingredients evenly.

5. Serve into individual bowls or one large bowl to share. Sprinkle with the nori and drizzle over dark soy sauce to taste.

POKE

TUNA WITH AVOCADO DRESSED WITH CITRUSY SOY SAUCE

This rice bowl dish is inspired by the Hawaiian delicacy poke (pronounced POH-keh), which began life as a fisherman's treat and used up the fresh fish trimmings from the catch of the day. Poke means 'to slice or cut', hence the fish is diced and placed on top of the bowl of rice. Here is my version of tuna tataki poke – the seared tuna has an excellent flavour and goes well with the citrus-fresh soy sauce. A perfect dish for a Hawaiian-like sunny day!

SERVES 4

1 avocado, peeled and stoned
freshly squeezed juice of 1 lime
800 g (5 cups) seasoned brown
   sushi rice (cooked weight, see
   pages 22–24)
1 shallot or red onion, finely
   chopped and soaked in water
a handful of mixed salad leaves
2 tablespoons shallot chips
   (optional)

TUNA

1 tablespoon grated garlic
1 tablespoon grated ginger
2 tablespoons vegetable oil
500 g (1 lb 2 oz) sashimi-quality
   tuna steaks
sea salt and freshly ground black
   pepper

DRESSING

4 tablespoons rice vinegar
4 tablespoons light soy sauce
4 tablespoons mirin
4 teaspoons toasted sesame oil
freshly squeezed juice of 1 lime
1 teaspoon sugar
a pinch of salt

1. To prepare the tuna, in a small bowl mix together the garlic, ginger and oil. Spread this onto both sides of each tuna steak, then season with the salt and pepper.

2. Heat a griddle pan to hot and sear the tuna steaks for 1 minute on each side for rare.

3. Let the tuna cool down, then cut it into 2-cm (¾-in) cubes.

4. To make the dressing, combine all the ingredients.

5. Cut the avocado into large cubes, then squeeze the lime juice over to prevent the flesh going brown.

6. Place the brown sushi rice in bowls and top with the tuna cubes, avocado, shallot or red onion and mixed leaves. Pour the dressing over the top just before serving. Top with shallot chips, if using, for extra crunch.

POKE

SALMON WITH AVOCADO AND SESAME DRESSING

This dish is the Hawaiian version of the Japanese donburi and is arguably Hawaii's favourite food. Poke is simply diced fish mixed with sushi rice and vegetables. It is a dish for the hot days of summer, where you'll feel refreshed just by the sight of it! This is a popular poke recipe using pieces of raw fish – the salmon melts in the mouth and blends deliciously with the other ingredients.

SERVES 4

1 tablespoon toasted sesame oil
2 tablespoons vegetable oil
1 tablespoon flaked (slivered) almonds
2 garlic cloves, thinly sliced
2 teaspoons finely chopped ginger
3 tablespoons dark soy sauce
2 tablespoons mirin
2 tablespoons toasted white sesame seeds
800 g (5 cups) seasoned sushi rice (cooked weight, see pages 22–23)
500 g (1 lb 2 oz) sashimi-quality salmon, cut into cubes (see page 14)
1 avocado, cut into 2-cm (¾-in) cubes and tossed in 1 teaspoon freshly squeezed lemon juice to stop them going brown
2 red radishes, thinly sliced
sesame dressing (see page 41)
a handful of salad leaves

1. Place the sesame oil and vegetable oil in a saucepan over a medium heat. When it becomes hot (but not at high smoking point), add the almonds and garlic and fry until golden. If you can, tilt the pan to gather the oil in one corner of the pan as this helps to cook evenly and quickly. Take care not to burn the garlic or almonds or they will become bitter.

2. Turn off the heat and remove the garlic chips and almonds from the pan. Drain the oil from the pan with paper towels.

3. Add the ginger to the pan while the oil is still hot. The ginger will cook in the residual heat.

4. When the oil has cooled down, add the dark soy sauce, mirin and toasted sesame seeds.

5. Place the sushi rice in a bowl, top with cubed salmon, avocado, and red radishes. Add the salad leaves and pour the dressing over the top just before serving.

SUSHI SALAD JAR

SALMON

This recipe was inspired by New York restaurant Ancolie, which only serves dishes in eco-friendly jars, where the food is beautiful to look at and delicious to eat. This multi-layered salad is the perfect dish to take on a picnic or even to the office for your lunch. Have fun making your own version and play with colours by using different vegetables, fish and sauces. For maximum freshness, eat this within one day. The longer you wait, the more the fish will 'cook' due to contact with the sauce, but it will still make a delicious ceviche-style salad.

SERVES 4
(IN FOUR 480-ML/16-OZ JARS)

300 g (10½ oz) sashimi-quality
    salmon, diced
150 g (5 oz) cooked prawns (shrimp)
12 red radishes, diced
160 g (1 cup) sweetcorn
    (corn kernels)
160 g (5½ oz) cucumber, diced
160 g (1¼ cups) edamame beans
400 g (2½ cups) seasoned brown
    sushi rice (cooked weight, see
    pages 22–24)
salad leaves or wild rocket (arugula)

PONZU JELLY
1 sheet of gelatine
3 tablespoons rice vinegar
3 tablespoons mirin
1 teaspoon clear raw honey
3 tablespoons usukuchi shoyu
    (light soy sauce)
1 tablespoon freshly squeezed
    lime juice

1. To make the ponzu jelly (jello), soak the gelatine sheet in a small bowl of water. Set aside.

2. Place the rice vinegar, honey, mirin and 100 ml (scant ½ cup) water in a medium saucepan, then bring it gently to the boil over a medium heat, simmering until the honey has dissolved.

3. Pour into a glass jug (pitcher) and add the light soy sauce. Squeeze in the lime juice and add the soaked gelatine, stirring well until it has melted.

4. Leave the jelly (jello) to cool down, then refrigerate for at least 3 hours to set. This should be a loose jelly (jello) texture as it stays at the bottom of the jar and binds well with the ingredients.

5. Once it has set, stir the jelly (jello) with a spoon to break it up, then divide it between the base of four clean, wide-mouthed jars. Add the salmon pieces, cooked prawns (shrimp), then layers of colourful vegetables. Top with the brown sushi rice and salad leaves or wild rocket (arugula).

6. Keep in a fridge until ready to serve, then tip into a bowl or plate to allow the sauce to season the salad.

SUSHI SALAD JAR
CHICKEN

The possibilities are endless with these jarred sushi salads! For this particular recipe, I decided to play with colours and shapes, with the cut okra resembling stars and the multi-grain rice taking on a lovely rosy hue thanks to the black rice grains. The chicken is dipped in my signature creamy sesame sauce, which makes it so flavoursome. This sauce goes perfectly well with any kind of salad. Simply swap the okra for broccoli or green beans if you prefer.

SERVES 4
(IN FOUR 480-ML/16-OZ JARS)

350 g (12 oz) boneless chicken breasts, skinless
12 quail's eggs
1 carrot, cut into julienne
½ red or yellow (bell) pepper, diced
12 okra, blanched and sliced into rounds
½ courgette (zucchini), cut into julienne or spiralled
400 g (2½ cups) seasoned multi-grain sushi rice (cooked weight, see pages 22–24)
a handful of mixed salad leaves

CREAMY SESAME DRESSING
3 tablespoons sesame paste (light tahini)
3 tablespoons usukuchi shoyu (light soy sauce)
3 tablespoons mirin
1½ tablespoons rice vinegar
1 tablespoon saikyo miso (white sweet smooth miso)
1 garlic clove, grated
1 shallot, finely chopped

1. To make the sesame dressing, mix the sesame paste with the light soy sauce until smooth. Add the mirin, stir until well combined, then mix in all the other seasonings. I suggest using a hand mixer or food processor to make a smooth dressing.

2. Bring a saucepan of water to the boil, add the chicken breasts and boil over a low heat for about 10 minutes until cooked through. Remove from the pan and allow to cool, then tear by hand into bite-sized pieces.

3. Place the eggs in a pan of boiling water and boil for 4 minutes. Remove from the pan and cool in cold water. When cool, shell them and then slice in half.

4. Divide the sauce between the base of four clean, wide-mouthed jars. Add the chicken, followed by layers of vegetables and eggs. Finish with a layer of sushi rice and salad leaves.

5. Keep in the fridge until ready to serve, then tip into a bowl or plate to allow the sesame dressing to season the salad.

野菜寿司

VEGETARIAN & VEGAN SUSHI

INARI SUSHI
RICE-FILLED FRIED TOFU SKINS

Inari sushi are juicy, sweet and salty pouches of abura age (fried tofu), typically stuffed with sesame seeds and sushi rice. I also add pickled ginger and shiso leaves for a stronger flavour accent. Their name comes from the Shinto god Inari, whose messengers are fried tofu-loving foxes! Enjoy on their own, or combine with other sushi, such as chirashi sushi.

MAKES 12 PIECES

6 abura age (fried thin tofu)
3 tablespoons sake
2 tablespoons sugar
2 tablespoons mirin
3 tablespoons dark soy sauce
450 g (2¾ cups) seasoned sushi rice
   (cooked weight, see pages 22–23)
1 tablespoon white sesame seeds
40 g (1½ oz) pickled ginger, finely
   chopped
12 purple baby shiso leaves
   (if available, or use green shiso)

1. Wash the abura age (fried tofu) in a bowl of boiling water to remove the oil on their surface.

2. Cut them in half. Using a chopstick (or rolling pin), roll over the top of the tofu to squeeze out the excess water – this pressure will help to separate the inner pouch skins to make a pocket.

3. Put the sake, sugar, mirin and dark soy sauce in a saucepan with 200 ml (1 scant cup) water and bring to the boil.

4. Add the tofu into the pan and bring back to the boil, then reduce the heat to low. Place a circle of baking parchment on top of the tofu and top with a small plate to act as a weight and stop the tofu swelling up. Simmer for 15 minutes, turning them over halfway through to season evenly. Take care when handling the plate as it will become very hot (alternatively, use a smaller saucepan lid as the handle will make it easier to remove).

5. Remove the pan from the heat and leave the tofu to cool down in the liquid.

6. Gently mix the sushi rice with the sesame seeds and pickled ginger.

7. Remove the tofu pouches from the liquid. To fill them, divide and shape the sushi rice into 12 even-sized oval shapes and stuff one into each fried tofu pouch. Top with a shiso leaf. Fold the flap of the tofu over the opening, then serve with the flap-side down.

VEGETARIAN NIGIRI

Vegetarian sushi have never looked more attractive than with this selection, and I bet you can tempt any confirmed meat or fish eater to dig in with gusto! Not only do they look stylish, but they are also truly delicious.

MISO AUBERGINE NIGIRI

MAKES 24 PIECES

1 aubergine (eggplant)
3 tablespoons rice bran oil
360 g (2¼ cups) seasoned sushi rice (cooked weight, see pages 22–23)
miso dengaku sauce (see page 41)
24 basil leaves

1. Cut the aubergine (eggplant) into slices 1 cm (½ in) thick. Cut into a half-moon shapes if using a wide aubergine (eggplant).

2. Heat the oil in a frying pan (skillet), add the aubergine (eggplant) slices and brown each side. Drain off any excess oil on a paper towel.

3. Wet your hand in water to stop the rice sticking it. This makes it much easier to handle the rice. Take a tablespoon (15 g/½ oz) of sushi rice and gently shape it to form a small oval ball. Repeat to make 24 balls.

4. Top the rice with a slice of aubergine (eggplant), then garnish with miso dengaku and a basil leaf.

ASPARAGUS NIGIRI

MAKES 24 PIECES

1 tablespoon vegetable oil
24 asparagus spears
360 g (2¼ cups) seasoned sushi rice (cooked weight, see pages 22–23)
1 sheet of nori, cut into 24 long ribbons (see point 4 on page 29)

DRESSING
2 tablespoons dark soy sauce
2 tablespoons mirin
1 teaspoon wasabi paste

1. Mix the dressing ingredients together in a bowl. Set aside.

2. Heat the oil in a frying pan (skillet), then add the asparagus and brown them. While the asparagus is still hot, toss with the dressing in a bowl. Leave to cool down.

3. Drain the seasonings and cut the asparagus into 5-cm (2-in) lengths, like penne pasta.

4. Wet your hand in water to stop the rice sticking to it. Take a tablespoon (15 g/½ oz) of rice and gently shape it to form a small oval ball. Repeat to make 24 balls.

5. Top the rice with asparagus and tie with nori ribbon.

BABY CORN NIGIRI

MAKES 24 PIECES

1 tablespoon vegetable oil
24 baby corn
360 g (2¼ cups) seasoned sushi rice (cooked weight, see pages 22–23)
1 sheet of nori, cut into 24 long ribbons (see point 4 on page 29)
teriyaki sauce (see page 38)

1. Heat the oil in a frying pan (skillet), then add the baby corn and brown them. Set aside to cool.

2. Butterfly the corn lengthwise from one end, keeping the tip joined.

3. Wet your hand in water to stop the rice sticking to it. This makes it much easier to handle the rice. Take a tablespoon (15 g/½ oz) of sushi rice and gently shape it to form a small oval ball. Repeat to make 24 balls.

5. Top the rice with baby corn and tie with nori ribbon. Thicken the teriyaki sauce by simmering it in a pan for 2–3 minutes, then brush the corn with the thickened teriyaki sauce.

PICKLED TURNIP TEMARI

MAKES 24 PIECES

2 baby turnips
1 pickled beetroot (beet)
**360 g (2¼ cups) seasoned sushi
  rice (cooked weight, see
  pages 22–23)**

PICKLING SEASONINGS
2 tablespoons rice vinegar
1 tablespoon agave
½ teaspoon salt
1 teaspoon rose water (optional)

1. Peel and very thinly slice the
turnips, using a mandoline slicer.

2. Put them into a small resealable
plastic bag and add the pickling
seasonings, 1 tablespoon water
and rose water for fragrance,
if using. Pickle for at least
20 minutes or up to 2 hours.

3. Remove from the pickling
seasonings and drain well on
a paper towel.

4. Roll the beetroot (beet) on
the rice to tint the rice a pale
pink colour like cherry blossom.
Remove the beetroot (beet) from
the rice before the pink becomes
too intense!

5. Wet your hand in water to stop
the rice sticking to it. This makes
it much easier to handle the rice.
Take a tablespoon (15 g/½ oz)
of sushi rice and gently shape
it to a small round ball. Repeat
to make 24 balls. Place the
slices of turnip on top.

MOCK SUSHI

Simple and easy to make (see the photo on the previous page), you'll have fun impressing your friends with these 'mock sushi' and tricking them with your veggie imitations of traditional sushi, such as using potato and nori instead of unagi (eel) or butternut squash instead of uni (sea urchin).

NORI POTATO TEMARI
MOCK EEL KABAYAKI

MAKES 24 PIECES

300 g (10½ oz) baking potato
1 sheet of nori, cut into 3-cm (1½-in) squares (see point 5 on page 29)
vegetable oil, for deep frying
360 g (2¼ cups) seasoned brown sushi rice (cooked weight, see pages 22-24)
wasabi paste
kabayaki sauce (see page 38)
24 pink peppercorns

1. Peel and finely grate the baking potato. Drain off any excess water. (Do not worry if the potato flesh turns brown.)

2. Heat the oil in a deep, heavy-based saucepan over a medium heat to 170°C (340°F).

3. Spread the potato paste thinly on the rough side of a square of nori using a butter knife. Score the surface of potato so it looks like eel skin (see photo on the previous page).

4. Deep-fry the potato at once with the nori side down. When the surface of potato has become brown, turn over a few times. Drain the excess oil.

5. To shape the temari, wet your hand in water to stop the rice sticking it and make 24 balls. Top with the fried potato, nori-side down. Put a dab of wasabi paste between the rice and nori to hold them together.

6. Drizzle the kabayaki sauce on the potato and top with a pink peppercorn.

ERYNGII NIGIRI
MOCK SCALLOP

MAKES 24 PIECES

4 eryngii mushrooms
2 tablespoons vegetable oil
1 sheet of nori, cut into 24 long ribbons (see page 29)
yuzu kosho paste (see page 38)
teriyaki sauce (see page 38)
360 g (2¼ cups) seasoned sushi rice (see pages 22-23)

1. Slice the eryngii into rounds 2-cm (¾-in) thick, then score the surface of eryngii into a grid pattern.

2. Heat the oil in a frying pan (skillet), then add the eryngii to brown them. Drain on paper towels.

3. Leave them to cool down, then butterfly-cut the eryngii from the sides to open them out.

4. Wet your hand in water to stop the rice sticking to it. This makes it much easier to handle the rice. Take a tablespoon (15 g / ½ oz) of sushi rice and gently shape it into a small oval ball. Repeat to make 24 balls.

5. Put a dab of yuzu kosho paste on the rice and top with eryngii. Tie with nori ribbon. Brush with the thickened teriyaki sauce.

BUTTERNUT SQUASH GUNKAN MAKI
MOCK SEA URCHIN

MAKES 24 PIECES

500 g (1 lb 2 oz) butternut squash
2 tablespoons vegetable oil
2 shallots
sea salt
1 teaspoon ground cumin
1 teaspoon ground coriander seeds
2–3 tablespoons dashi stock or
    water
4 sheets of nori, cut into long strips,
    along the lines (see point 3 on
    page 29)
10-cm (4-in) piece of cucumber,
    thinly sliced into half moons
360 g (2¼ cups) seasoned sushi rice
    (cooked weight, see pages 22–23)
soy sauce, to serve

1. Preheat the oven to 180°C (350°F) Gas 4.

2. Peel and dice the squash, Rub in the oil, along with the shallots, then put on a baking tray and bake in the preheated oven for about 15 minutes or until softened.

3. Leave to cool, then mash them in a bowl (or use a food processor) to make a smooth paste. Blend in the salt and spices, and add dashi or water if it is too thick (the mixture should hold its shape). Spoon into a piping bag.

4. Wet your hand in water to stop the rice sticking to it. This makes it much easier to handle the rice. Take a tablespoon (15 g/½ oz) of sushi rice and gently shape it into a small oval ball. Repeat to make 24 balls.

5. Wrap each rice ball with a nori strip. Stick a grain of sushi rice onto the end of the nori to seal. Place the cucumber slices at the back of nori, then pipe the squash paste to fill the space.

6. Serve them straight away with soy sauce. (The nori becomes soggy if you leave it too long.)

PEPPER NIGIRI
MOCK TUNA

MAKES 24 PIECES

2 red (bell) peppers (you could
    also use yellow or orange)
1 tablespoon vegetable oil
360 g (2¼ cups) seasoned sushi
    rice (cooked weight, see pages
    22–23)
2 teaspoons ume paste
    (see page 18)
snipped chives
soy sauce, to serve

PICKLING SEASONINGS
120 ml (½ cup) mirin
120 ml (½ cup) rice vinegar
a pinch of sea salt

1. Preheat the grill (broiler) to high (200°C/400°F).

2. To make the red (bell) pepper topping, cut the peppers into quarters, Remove the seeds and white parts inside the pepper, then coat the skin lightly in oil.

3. Place the pepper skin side up on a foil-covered baking tray and grill (broil) for 12 minutes until the skin blisters, but do not burn the skin as this will discolour the flesh.

4. Wrap the peppers in the foil to steam, then unwrap and peel off the skins.

5. Mix together the pickling seasonings in a bowl. Add the peppers and let them pickle for at least 20 minutes or overnight.

6. Wipe off the seasoning gently from the peppers, then cut into 3 x 7-cm (1¼ x 2¾-in) rectangles.

7. Wet your hand in water to stop the rice sticking to it. This makes it much easier to handle the rice. Take a tablespoon (15 g/½ oz) of sushi rice and gently shape it to a small oval ball. Repeat to make 24 balls.

8. Top the rice with red pepper, ume paste and chives. Serve with soy sauce.

URAMAKI
FLAVOURSOME VEGETARIAN ROLL

So often I have found that the only vegetarian fillings for sushi rolls are cucumber or avocado, which becomes very boring. Here I use tenderstem broccoli (broccolini) which is deep fried in oil, creating a light crunchiness and aromatic flavour, and okra, which has a distinctive texture. This combination of vegetables provides a unique and pleasing flavour sensation. As a topping, I have added spiced butternut squash and chilli cress for more exotic flavours.

MAKES 4 ROLLS

vegetable oil, for deep frying
400 g (2½ cups) seasoned multi-grain sushi rice (cooked weight, see pages 22–24)
2 sheets of nori, cut in half
soy sauce, to serve

FILLINGS
4 tenderstem broccoli (broccolini)
½ avocado, sliced lengthways into 8, with 1 teaspoon fresh lime juice drizzled over
½ carrot, cut into fine matchsticks
4 okra, blanched, cut in half lengthways
4 teaspoons spicy yuzu mayo (see page 41)

OPTIONAL TOPPINGS
butternut squash paste (see page 155)
chilli cress or baby cress

1. Remove any leaves from the broccoli (broccolini) stems as they would sizzle when deep fried. Dry the surface of the broccoli.

2. Heat the oil in a medium saucepan to 180°C/ 350°F. Deep fry the broccoli for 1 minute, adjusting the heat between medium and high to maintain the correct temperature. Turn them over and fry for another 1 minute. Remove from the oil and drain on paper towels or a baking rack.

3. Cover a bamboo mat with clingfilm (plastic wrap) to stop the sushi rice sticking (see page 32). Place the nori (rough side up) at the front of the mat.

4. Wet your hand in water to stop the rice sticking to it. Take an apple-sized amount (100 g/3½ oz) of sushi rice and spread evenly to completely cover the nori. Turn the nori and rice over carefully. On the centre of the nori, place your fillings in a line.

5. Start rolling! Hold the bamboo mat and nori with rice, then fold the near edge of the nori. Leave about 1.5 cm (¾ in) of blank space at the other end of nori, be careful not to move the fillings in the centre of the roll, then press the rice along the bamboo mat. Unroll the mat and use it to roll the rest of the nori.

6. To cut the roll, wipe a knife with a wet towel – this helps to cut the roll cleanly so repeat for each cut. Cut across the centre of the roll, then line the two pieces up side by side and cut each piece into four.

7. Top with the squash paste and garnish with cress. Serve with soy sauce.

INDEX

Designers Megan Smith and Barbara Zuñiga
Editors Alice Sambrook and Gillian Haslam
Art Director Leslie Harrington
Editorial Director Julia Charles
Production Controller Gordana Simakovic
Publisher Cindy Richards
Food Stylist Atsuko Ikeda
Prop Stylist Tony Hutchinson
Indexer Hilary Bird
Illustrator Jasmin Sohi

Published in 2017 by
Ryland Peters & Small
20-21 Jockey's Fields
London WC1R 4BW
and
341 East 116th Street
New York, NY 10029

www.rylandpeters.com

10 9 8 7 6 5 4

Text © Atsuko Ikeda 2017

Design, illustration and
commissioned photography
© Ryland Peters & Small 2017

ISBN 978-1-84975-884-0

A CIP record for this book
is available from the Brisih
Library. US Library of Congress
CIP data has been applied for.

Printed in China

Notes
· Both British (Metric) and
American (Imperial plus US
cups) measurements are
included in these recipes for
your convenience. However it
is important to work with one
set of measurements and not
alternate between the two
within a recipe.
· All spoon measurements
are level unless otherwise
specified.

· Uncooked or partially cooked
eggs should not be served
to the very old, frail, young
children, pregnant women
or those with compromised
immune systems.
· When following a recipe which
uses raw fish or meat, always
ensure you buy sashimi-quality
ingredients and use on the day
of purchase. Raw fish or meat
should not be served to the
very old, frail, young children,
pregnant women or those with
compromised immune systems,
without medical advice.
· Ovens should be preheated
to the specified temperatures.
We recommend using an
oven thermometer. If using
a fan-assisted oven, adjust
temperatures according to the
manufacturer's instructions.
· When a recipe calls for the
grated zest of citrus fruit, buy
unwaxed fruit and wash well
before using. If you can only
find treated fruit, scrub well in
warm soapy water before using.

Food Safety Notice
The information contained
within this book is intended
as a general guide to sushi-
making at home based on the
author's recipe development
and experience. Although
all reasonable care has been
taken in the preparation of this
book, neither the publishers
nor the author can accept any
liability for any consequence
from the use thereof, or the
information contained therein.
Please consult an up-to-date
government source on food
safety for further information.

ACKNOWLEDGEMENTS

I am so grateful to the wonderful team at my publishers, Ryland Peters & Small and I appreciate you giving me this opportunity to write my first cookbook. Cindy Richards, Alice Sambrook especially (who made this happen!), Leslie Harrington, Megan Smith, Julia Charles and Gillian Haslam – thanks to all of you for your dedicated hard work in making this book so stunning.

The book would not look so beautiful without the incredibly creative team. Yuki Sugiura, your talented eyes are magical, it has been super amazing to work with you and I have learned so much from you during the photoshoots. Tony Hutchinson, I am always impressed by your dedicated work, and the props you selected made my sushi look so gorgeous. Jasmin Sohi, you have created an elegant yet stylish infographic, making this book unique. Thank you for all of your professional work on this book.

Special gratitude to my friends who shared this journey with me from the beginning to the end. Elsa Gleeson, my dear friend, ultra mum of two children, your endless encouragement and sister-like support for me have been an enormous influence during this book process. Adding your artistic sense of humour has made this book even more enjoyable to read. Noriko Tanaka, I am so fortunate to be friends with you and it is inspiring to work with you. Your generous support and expert advice have given me depth. You are my star!

Thanks to all my friends and assistants who contributed to the creation of this book, including Yokichi Seno (at Kataba) for the Japanese props and for sharing your knowledge of the knives.

I appreciate all my students, who have made me realise that the world of sushi can appeal to all.

Lastly, to my family. For giving me love, believing in me, being proud of me, I thank my parents Yuriko and Hideki Ikeda in Japan. Michele Rossi, my husband, always supportive, patient, creative, critical and emotional! I am even more emotional than you when I think of this adventure, amore. I would not have been able to go through this without your help. I am always thankful that you are a great dad to Nicolo and I am so proud that we achieved this goal together!